KAREN L. MAPP, ILENE CARVER, AND J...

POWERFUL PARTNERSHIPS

*A Teacher's Guide
to Engaging Families
for Student Success*

📖 SCHOLASTIC

ACKNOWLEDGMENTS

The writing of this book would not be possible without the school staff, teachers, parents, researchers, and many other education professionals who shared with us their stories, expertise, and ideas. We want to thank them for their generous contributions and for the work they are doing to build the critical partnerships between families and schools.

Specifically, we are deeply grateful for the generosity of time from the following individuals and their contributions to our book: Dara Bayer, Naomi Bones, Michele Brooks, Rebecca Brown, Sonya Brown, Meg Bruton, Melissa Bryant, Elizabeth Canada, Judy Carson, Sabine Ferdinand, Emma Fialka-Feldman, Nachelle Gordon, Dr. William Henderson, Dr. Soo Hong, Chandra Joseph-Lacet, Rosa Larez, Jamila Nichols, Dwayne Nunez, Myriam Ortiz, Carrie Rose, Maya Sanchez, Aracelis Santana, Lindsay Slabich, Camelia Toussaint, Elizabeth Goncalves Wachman, Adrienne Wetmore, Kristen Whitaker, and Tierra Wooley.

We want to thank the team at Scholastic FACE, specifically Lois Bridges, for her eternal optimism, her patience, and her amazing dedication and championing of family partnerships. Thanks also to Ron Mirr, Brian LaRossa, and Tonya Leslie who provided guidance and contributions to the book.

Karen would like to thank Kidus Mezgebu, her faculty assistant, for taking care of our creative space needs as well as for his invaluable support whenever we ran into technical difficulties.

Finally, we—Karen, Jessica, and Ilene—want to thank our own families. We are continually sustained and inspired by our families who are our sounding boards, our support systems, and our biggest cheerleaders. This book could never have happened without your love and support.

CREDITS

Excerpt from *Beyond the Bake Sale* by Anne T. Henderson, Karen L. Mapp, Vivian R. Johnson, and Don Davies. Copyright © 2007 by Anne T. Henderson, Karen L. Mapp, Vivian R. Johnson, and Don Davies. The New Press. Excerpt from *The Essential Conversation: What Parents and Teachers Can Learn From Each Other* by Sara Lawrence-Lightfoot. Copyright © 2003 by Sara Lawrence-Lightfoot. Used by permission of Ballantine Books, an imprint of Random House Publishing Group, a division of Penguin Random House LLC. Excerpt from *Why Are All the Black Kids Sitting Together in the Cafeteria?* by Beverley Daniel Tatum, Ph.D. Copyright © 2003, 1999, 1997 by Beverley Daniel Tatum, Ph.D. Used by permission of Basic Books, a division of Perseus Books Group. "PTHV Model: The Core Practices (Our Non-Negotiables)" copyright © 2016 by Parent Teacher Home Visits. Retrieved from http://www.pthvp.org/what-we-do/pthv-model. Used by permission of Parent Teacher Home Visits.
All rights reserved.

Editor: Lois Bridges
Development/production editor: Danny Miller
Editorial director: Sarah Longhi
Editorial assistant manager: Suzanne Akceylan
Cover designer: Brian LaRossa
Interior designer: Maria Lilja

Contents

Build Your Case for Family Engagement

This book is written with you, the teacher, in mind, and begins with the premise that all teachers want to be and feel effective as teachers. Teachers want more than anything to see their students making progress academically, developmentally, and socially. We know that you, as a teacher, feel a sense of well-being and accomplishment when:

- your students are engaged and excited by what they are learning in class and are motivated to practice what they have learned.

- all of your students are showing growth in academic and social-emotional benchmarks and have in some way made steady progress.

- you see their progress reflected in student data as well as in your observations of them in the classroom.

- your students feel more connected to their peers, their teachers, and their school community.

In order for you to achieve the best possible results for your students, we know certain factors have to be present. Your school has to be led by a leader who is competent and is a positive driver of change; you need to be surrounded by colleagues who are skilled and competent; you need to receive great instructional guidance and support; and there must be very strong ties with the families and community members that your school serves. All of these "ingredients" have to be present and working together for your school to run well and for your students to have successful outcomes (Bryk, 2010).

This book focuses on the ingredient that has to do with your relationships with the families of the children that you teach. We want to make the case that partnership with families is not only important to maximize student learning, but is also a key factor in your own well-being and success as a teacher.

The research is resounding—creating meaningful partnerships with parents will help your students succeed both academically and socially. Here is what the research tells us: When parents are engaged and involved, their children succeed (Henderson & Mapp, 2002). Specifically:

- Their children's grades go up.
- They attend school more regularly.
- They are more likely to enroll in higher-level programs.
- They are more likely to graduate and go on to college.
- They are more excited and positive about school and learning.
- They have fewer discipline issues inside and outside class.

With such far-reaching effects, we believe engaging parents is essential for the short- and long-term success of your students. We hope to provide you with the necessary tools to create such partnerships in your own classrooms.

Ilene Carver

NOTE FROM ILENE

Jorge's* reading progress.

Ilene tells this story about a student in her second-grade class:

Jorge entered our second-grade classroom as a new student to the school. He is an English Learner, and Spanish is the language spoken at home. When Jorge arrived, he didn't yet know any of the sounds that letters make. On a reading assessment in late September, he scored at an early kindergarten level. At the mid-October family conference, both Jorge and his mother were in tears. It was devastating to be seven years old and not to be able to read. During the conference, Jorge set a goal to improve his reading. He pledged to read every chance he got, and his mother promised to sit with Jorge each night and to listen to him read. Jorge joined a reading intervention group at school, and I sent home many books for him to read, exchanging the books as he mastered them. In less than two months, Jorge could identify all the sounds the letters make, and he had increased his reading by two levels. In late November, Jorge was reading at an end-of-kindergarten level—with six months of the school year still ahead. At the next family conference, Jorge's mother spoke about how she renewed her commitment to listen to Jorge read at home once she understood its importance. Without a doubt, Jorge's ability to make reading progress was multiplied by the home-school connection.

(*Note that the names of students have been changed in this book except in anecdotes written by parents about their own children.)

As many of our schools are rich with students of diverse cultures, languages, and backgrounds, we believe these family relationships are even more important. We know that such diversity comes with great benefits, and can also include its own challenges for building effective family partnerships; we also believe that creating these relationships is essential for building the most vibrant learning communities. In this book, we intend to address these challenges and provide you with effective strategies.

Overall, we aim to help you engage with families in ways that support student academic achievement, your success as a teacher, and the overall improvement of your school. Before you dive into the rest of the book, you might already have a few questions for us....

Q What happens if my school leader isn't on board?

A Teachers often ask us the following question: What do you do if your school leader isn't enthusiastic or supportive about engaging families? Even if you are in a school that does not have strong institutional structures and supports around family engagement, strengthening your partnerships with families is still worthwhile to pursue. Again, we have learned that family engagement is critical not only to student achievement but also to *your well-being as a teacher*. Let's face it, partnering with families is indeed harder to accomplish without the institutional culture and support, but you can *still* accomplish quite a bit on your own to intentionally build relationships of trust and respect with the families of the children that you teach. Change doesn't always start at the top. Creating a model in your classroom of what true family engagement looks like could have a profound impact on helping change your school's mindset toward partnering with parents. Your effectiveness as a teacher is profoundly affected by these partnerships.

Q Okay, but I already have so much on my plate!

We ask you to keep an open mind as you read this book, as we may be suggesting ways of thinking about and engaging with families that may be new, different, and, perhaps, a little unsettling. With all that you already have going on, and with all of the pressure already being placed on teachers, you may be understandably skeptical about an additional strategy to try.

It may seem counterintuitive to you, but we have learned from many teachers that the "extra" work they put in to partner with families ultimately *decreases* their workload and makes their jobs more enjoyable and fulfilling. Indeed, research shows that teachers stay at schools where they have strong partnerships with the families of their students (Allensworth, Ponisciak & Mazzeo, 2009). We will ask you to reconsider traditional ways of thinking about families and the role family members play in their children's education. It has been our experience that some districts and schools see families and community members as entities to be *managed* and held at bay instead of *welcomed* as full partners in reaching the teaching and learning goals of our schools and students. As teachers, we are always looking for powerful partners with whom to collaborate, whether they are other teachers, afterschool partners, or administrators. Our goal with this book is to help you cultivate powerful partnerships with families, as co-creators of excellent educational opportunities for their children and their children's classrooms.

Q Sure, but what if my parents don't seem to have time?

A Not every parent will be able to participate in the typical "parent activities"—attending the parent-teacher organization meetings, baking goods for the fundraiser, or helping out with a school play or field trip. But even if they can't, that doesn't mean they don't want to be involved and that they can't contribute to their child's academic success.

Throughout this book, we will ask you to expand your definition of what successful engagement and partnership might and can look like. Traditionally, schools focus on family engagement activities that only work for a certain group of families—often families who have means and the extra time or flexibility to be present at school.

There are many factors that can make it hard to participate in these more traditional activities, from living far from the school and having no means to access the school easily, to working jobs that provide little flexibility to negotiate leave during the school day. But often families may already be deeply engaged at home and in their communities, and we hope to help you recognize and honor those many types of engagement.

Last, but not least, we have found that families will make the time when we really let them know *how important they are* to us as teachers and when we invite them to engage. Families have to hear this from you and know that you mean it.

NOTE FROM ILENE
Family Engagement and My Survival as a Teacher

Ilene Carver

Ilene describes the impact of family engagement on her first year of teaching.

In my first year of teaching, reaching out to families was a matter of survival. I remember I had a wonderful group of children with many challenges. I'm convinced that my ability to successfully teach those students had a lot to do with the support I had from families. That support was a result of the time I put into building relationships. There is no doubt that it meant a lot to my students that their mom, dad, grandma, uncle, and sometimes several of these people and I had a close and connected relationship. What happened at home and what happened at school were not two different worlds.

You will find that your families can serve as a lifeline for you, and having families as your partners can make the practice of teaching more enjoyable and fulfilling.

Q What if we don't speak the same language?

There is no doubt that this is a challenge, but with some creativity and help from others, these families can and must be reached. Indeed, evidence shows that families for whom English is not the first language (English Learners, or ELs) are very interested in being engaged in their children's education. (Lopez, 2001; Zacarian, 2011). Remember, not speaking English doesn't mean that your families aren't interested in or passionate about their children's academic and emotional success. Remember, too, that while it might be initially harder to communicate with them, these parents have a lot to contribute to your success as a classroom teacher.

We realize that for some of you, your school communities are facing large demographic shifts. These changes will ultimately require you, your school, and your district to come together and decide how you will support communicating and partnering with families who speak languages that are not spoken by you or your colleagues. But, for you individually, we'll provide some helpful suggestions throughout the book for how to connect with your families whose first language is not English.

Whom This Book Is For

We have written this book primarily for you, the teacher. Realizing that teaching strategies and goals are not identical for all teachers, we have tried to anticipate and address the varied needs of both novices and veterans and of teachers spanning grades Pre-K through 12. In addition, we hope this book will help administrators trying to foster strong engagement practices in their school's classrooms. More specifically:

If you are…

- A beginning teacher, we can help you begin to shape your practice, weaving in strategies that will serve you throughout your teaching career.

- An experienced teacher, we hope to help transform and add to your practice, providing you with important skills and ideas to incorporate into your arsenal.

If you are…

- A pre-K or elementary school teacher, we can help you start families on their partnership journey with schools and teachers, and build their confidence to be engaged in their child's learning and development right from the start. You can be the catalyst for early trust and respect between families and their schools, and can break down historical barriers that may already exist between your families and institutions like schools.

- A middle or high school teacher, we can help you both shape your practice and provide you with ideas to engage parents at a time in their students' education when, most typically, schools and parents are likely to go their separate ways. We know from research that middle and high school students do want and need their parents' support and that their support will help them succeed.

If you are…

- A principal or school administrator, we can provide you with a road map for developing and honing the essential skills your teachers will need to succeed. We can help you build the kinds of support and strategies to help your staff succeed in creating and sustaining partnerships. We can also help you develop the institutional and organizational practices to support home-school partnerships throughout your school.

How This Book Is Organized

Throughout the book, we will share stories from practitioners and others along with practical tips and anecdotes (like the "Notes" from Ilene about her students, Jorge and Michael) from teachers, school leaders, parents, and researchers that explore how to adapt and strengthen your partnerships with families. We will engage you in opportunities to think about and assess your own skills, knowledge, and dispositions—your core beliefs and values—when it comes to engaging families. This book is more about your approach to the work, rather than a checklist of practices and events (though we will provide a few ideas sprinkled throughout). We are confident that you will design even better events and initiatives after you read this book.

A note about our terminology: You will notice throughout the book that we use both "family/families" and "parent/parents" when referring to the important adult stakeholders in a child's life. We do prefer the term "family" as it is more inclusive and recognizes the role of grandparents, aunts and uncles, foster parents, and other kin who make a difference. We do switch back and forth—just know that we are always referring to the various adult stakeholders who support children's learning and development.

PARTNERSHIP CLIPS

Throughout the book, you'll see links to a series of Partnership Clips that you can access at www.scholastic.com/PartnerResources. Seven of the videos feature Dr. Karen Mapp addressing key issues and topics with video footage drawn from her Harvard presentations and her online class. In the Reflection section at the end of each chapter, you'll see clips of teachers and other family engagement advocates responding to the questions Dr. Mapp poses about family engagement. We hope these questions will spark your own family engagement reflections.

Chapter 1: Examine Your Core Beliefs

Becoming a skilled practitioner in the area of family partnerships doesn't start with an in-depth knowledge of the research on family partnerships or access to a bucket filled with activities and programs—it starts with YOU! Chapter 1 engages you in a conversation about your core beliefs about the role of families in the education of the students in your classroom.

Chapter 2: Harness the Power of Partnerships

We've already used the word *partnership* several times in this introduction. What exactly do we mean by partnerships with families? Besides offering up some descriptions of partnerships between home and school, we also share what we now know about the most effective way to build and sustain respectful partnerships with families.

Chapter 3: Welcome, Honor, and Connect With Your Families

How do you begin the important work of forming powerful partners with families? In Chapter 3, we dive into how to make your initial outreach to families and begin to build relationships at the beginning of the school year. We will discuss and detail impactful practices including home visits, phone calls home, and back-to-school nights.

Chapter 4: Transform Your Family Conferences and IEP Meetings

Having laid the foundation for partnering with families at the beginning of the year, how do you deepen these relationships as the year continues? In Chapter 4, we will look closely into two important types of conversations you are likely to have with families: Family-Teacher Conferences and Individualized Education Plan (IEP) Meetings. For each we will dive into strategies for how you might bring families more meaningfully into a working partnership.

Chapter 5: Maintain Strong Family Ties Throughout the Year

Throughout the year, there will be opportunities to learn from and partner with your students' families. In this chapter, we present you with the voices of four teachers from elementary, middle, and high school, each describing a different strategy, technique, or approach to further build these relationships.

Chapter 6: Support Your Work With Family-Friendly Resources

The tools, techniques, and most important, discussions around mindset we have presented in the book are only the beginning of a lifelong journey in this work. In this final chapter, we share additional tools for your classroom and practice that other practitioners and experts have shared with us. Luckily, too, there are many phenomenal organizations supporting the development of powerful partnerships between families and schools. We hope you will use these organizations and resources to further expand and build your own practice.

Ilene Carver

A Personal Reflection

In order to truly provide equitable and excellent learning opportunities for all our children, there is a lot we need to change in our society. I think teachers and all of us in the field of education need to state clearly that if we want to close the achievement gap across race and class, we need to ensure that ALL of our children and their families have sufficient food, shelter, employment opportunities, and health care (including mental health care), and work to stop the overrepresentation of people of color in our prisons and as victims of police crimes. It is critical that we stand together as educators to organize around these issues. At the same time, we know this is a fight we won't win tomorrow, or even this year.

As educators, we do have the power, right now, to decide what kinds of communities we build in our schools. This is something we can work on today, tomorrow, and next week. We can do a better job of educating our young people if we work toward dismantling the hierarchical relationship that often exists between school professionals and family members. We can replace it by building partnerships that enable families and school staff to see themselves as equals and as members of the same team, working their hardest to provide a first-class educational experience for all students.

Final Thoughts

Our goal is to strengthen your family engagement practice and, in doing so, strengthen your classroom success. We think this work is incredibly impactful—and want to share with you what we have learned about the best elements of partnering with families and how we hope it will transform your practice.

Partnering with families will:

- contribute to your sense of accomplishment as a teacher.
- reduce your feelings of isolation—your families can act as a source of strength for you as a community that supports your work and goals of student achievement.

- break down the race and class hierarchies that have historically dominated and prevented healthy and respectful family-school relationships.

- create a productive team of allies that surround and support the child and you as the teacher.

- cultivate mutual respect and trust between home and school—when challenges do arise, they are much more easily resolved.

- transform the instinct to be defensive and break down the us-versus-them dynamic.

We each come to this work with a different story, a different history, and different classroom experiences, all of which shape our approach to building partnerships. Perhaps your parents were constantly helping out in your own classroom, perhaps they never stepped foot inside. Perhaps you've had an incredibly rewarding conversation or interaction with the parent of one of your students, or perhaps you are right now recalling that time a parent yelled at you or canceled a long-set-up meeting. These stories shape us, and will be important initial stepping-stones as we ask you to consider and, perhaps, reconsider the role parents can play in your classroom.

PARTNERSHIP CLIP

Introduction: Your Colleagues Reflect

Listen to your colleagues reflect on their experiences with family engagment.

scholastic.com/PartnerResources

Reflection

Think of a time you partnered with a family to support a student in your classroom. What was the outcome for the student? For the family? What kind of impact did this partnership have on you and your teaching?

Examine Your Core Beliefs

Y ou are committed and excited to create strong partnerships with parents, but where do you start? We are certain that many of you might be saying, "I've already tried to encourage more family engagement with the parents of my students. In fact, our school has tried several techniques, and none of them have worked!"

It's frustrating to throw yourself into planning a family event, only to have a few parents attend. We understand that you may have tried offering incentives to parents (raffles and prizes), incentives to the class that brings in the most parents (pizza parties and special trips), home-baked treats, child care, and even transportation to events. We aren't saying that these strategies aren't important—they are, but there are other very important components necessary for building successful partnerships with families.

The first component, and the most important, is YOU.

What do you know about your students' lives? What do you know about their families? What assumptions might you have about their homes, communities, and educational values? These *core beliefs* (Henderson, Mapp, Johnson & Davies, 2007) impact your ability to build vibrant partnerships with families.

Throughout this book, we aim to enhance your skills, knowledge, and mindset to do this work well. For this first chapter, we want to focus on the disposition and beliefs required for you to partner effectively with families.

The Disposition to Partner Well

We are certain that you have experienced what it is like to work with colleagues who are truly welcoming to you, honor your presence, treat you like an equal, and believe in the work you are doing together. They are committed to developing a trusting and respectful working relationship with you, and you value their enthusiasm and enjoy working with them. You can tell by their actions and language that they believe that working and collaborating with you is not only important, but also enjoyable. They are not acting out of obligation; partnering with you is meaningful to them. You would describe them as authentic, transparent, respectful, and caring.

This way of being—a true partnership—is what families tell us they want to share with school staff. To develop this trusting and caring relationship with your families, you, as the practitioner, come to this work with a set of deeply grounded beliefs about the value of partnership with all of your families, regardless of the various differences between your background and theirs. Everything that you do or say to families—from how you make a phone call home to how you conduct a conference with a family—is greatly influenced by your inner core beliefs about your families, even if you don't always realize it.

Examining Your Beliefs About Family Engagement

We believe that the best place to begin this work is with self-examination. Much of what we do as practitioners is shaped by our beliefs and values, and your decisions about how to engage with families will be anchored by your beliefs about them and their communities.

PARTNERSHIP CLIP
Examining Your Core Beliefs Over Time

scholastic.com/PartnerResources

While we might not always recognize it, many past experiences, both positive and negative, shape our interactions with families. Your own family's experiences with your elementary school teacher; your memories of how welcoming your school was to you as a child; your previous conversations with parents of your students, strained or relaxed, all subtly affect how you will approach this work.

Examining our values and beliefs about family engagement is especially important when we are from different racial, ethnic, socioeconomic, and educational backgrounds from the families that our schools serve.

The biases and assumptions that we may have about the families of our children, left unexamined, can hamper our ability to create effective partnerships with them.

We don't expect that you will necessarily start this work with this mindset in place—this conviction is something that will grow over time. We hope that throughout this book you will engage with our ideas—and try our quick free-writes and assignments—and see if your beliefs about families begin to shift or evolve. We have come to see how essential this mindset is to building successful partnerships, and we hope you will, too.

Examine Your Own Beliefs

We realize the self-examination we've just described might sound daunting and perhaps even uncomfortable. How do you identify your biases and assumptions, particularly if they are, as we've said, not on the surface?

To do this, we suggest you start with this writing assignment: Reflect on the following questions. We hope you will be as honest and detailed as you can (no one else is going to read this).

1. Think back to your own childhood and own school experience. How was your family connected or not connected to your school and educational experience?
2. How might these past experiences, positive or negative, shape your beliefs as a teacher about family engagement?
3. What fears, hesitations, or apprehensions do you have about this work? What barriers will you have to overcome?
4. What passions, beliefs, and commitments do you bring that will help you do this work?

Family Engagement: Four Essential Core Beliefs

When Karen worked as Deputy Superintendent for Family and Student Engagement in Boston, she met a number of school leaders and teachers who were exemplary family engagement practitioners. Each spoke about having a set of beliefs that guided their work with families: that all families had hopes and dreams for their children, that families had the capacity to support their children's learning, that families were equal partners in the work of student and school improvement, and that, because of the history of less-than-positive relationships between families and school staff, school leaders and staff had to take the first step—to extend the first hand—to build partnerships with families.

These themes from conversations with these practitioners formed the basis for the essential Core Beliefs for Family Engagement outlined in Chapter 3 of *Beyond the Bake Sale: The Essential Guide to Family-School Partnerships* (Henderson et al., 2007).

PARTNERSHIP CLIP

The Four Essential Core Beliefs

scholastic.com/PartnerResources

THE FOUR ESSENTIAL CORE BELIEFS

1. **All families have dreams for their children and want the best for them.**

2. **All families have the capacity to support their children's learning.**

3. **Families and school staff are equal partners.**

4. **The responsibility for cultivating and sustaining partnerships among school, home, and community rests primarily with school staff, especially school leaders.**

Core Belief 1: All families have dreams for their children and want the best for them.

Parents and families want their children to succeed. They have high expectations for their son's or daughter's educational achievement, which is important to acknowledge and validate. We emphasize the *all* here, because at times, practitioners interpret family patterns and behaviors as not having hopes and dreams for their children's well-being and success. Poverty, mental health issues, housing, and other systemic and structural factors impact families' engagement in their children's education, but we've seen time and time again in our work with families that they DO care and want the best for their children.

The heart-dotted exclamation points, the expectations of excellence, the hopes for first and second grade in some very personal letters (see below), reflect the hopes and dreams Kai's, Nysia's, and Vismark's moms all have for their children. Every parent has such dreams.

"Hopes and Dreams" letters from parents

Rosa Lopez

Me gustaria que su hijo Vismark prosperara mucho en la escritura y en la lectura ya que estos son la base para un buen comienzo.

Me gustaria que aprendiera a respetar a los demas como asi mismo y que tenga mucha disiplina para que en mañana o el proximo año este mas capacitado y en el futuro triunfe como un buen Profecional.

Dear Kai,
I hope you achieve all of your goals in second grade. I want you to be the best scholar you can be. I hope at the end of this school year you will be reading a chapter book to Mommy, and telling me what time it is? I also hope you excel in math as that is your favorite subject.

Love my favorite girl.

Love
Mommy

Hi Nysia,

Mommy is so proud of you! My Hope for you in your 1st grade is that you enjoy Learning, and Daddy's Hope for you is that you know that you are Part of a large Community that loves you and is proud of you! WE LOVE YOU xoxo

You might be skeptical, thinking: "Sure, this is true for some families, but not all. My colleagues and I know parents who don't show up for Parent Night even after we've sent multiple invitations. We know parents who don't return our phone calls. We know families who are absent, abusive, drug-addicted, or in other ways don't seem to care at all about the well-being of their children."

Too often, teachers might see such parents and make the assumption that they "just don't care." Such conclusions are too often made about parents of color, parents who come from poor neighborhoods, or parents who have come here from other countries. What teachers and school staff don't often see or acknowledge are the challenges those families might be facing, the overwhelming struggles that might prevent them from taking a more active role in their child's education, as well as the past and current disrespectful and discriminatory interactions families may have experienced in schools.

Believing that parents aren't invested in their child's future because they don't seem to engage with the school couldn't be further from the truth. In her book about the complexities and dynamics of parent-teacher conferences, Sara Lawrence-Lightfoot states:

> *I believe that all parents hold big expectations for the role that schools will play in the life chances of their children. They all harbor a large wish list of dreams and aspirations for their youngsters. All families care deeply about their children's education and hope that their progeny will be happier, more productive, and more successful than they have been in their lives* (Lawrence-Lightfoot, 2003).

Ilene Carver

NOTE FROM ILENE AND JESSICA

Ilene and Jessica Share Their Thoughts About the Core Beliefs

If we as teachers absolutely believe in our souls that families want to support their children and will do everything they can to help them, and we communicate this, families will be involved. I have been teaching in the Boston Public Schools for more than 20 years, and I have yet to meet a family where there wasn't someone with whom I could build a relationship in support of their child's success."

~ Ilene

Jessica Lander

I teach English Learners; my students come from as far away as Cambodia, Brazil, and Lebanon. From time to time, I've heard some speak disparagingly about the parents of my students. "Oh, they just don't have the same understanding about education as we do," or "They just don't want the same thing for their children," or, most often, "Well, you see, in their culture they don't believe girls should go to college." I hear these statements and think of my students and their families, families who have traveled hundreds of miles, who have fled wars and abandoned homes because of bombings, who have survived for years in refugee camps and given up respected professions in their own country to start again in ours. They came here for opportunity. They came here to provide their children with a new and brighter future—I cannot think of a more powerful expression of how deeply these families value their child's educational success.

~ Jessica

Let us be clear: We—the authors of this book—have never met a parent who doesn't care about the future of his or her child, and we don't believe we ever will. As teachers, it is important to recognize that families, even those who are facing significant challenges, do have aspirations for their children and are usually looking to the schools to help make those aspirations come true.

Core Belief 2: All families have the capacity to support their children's learning.

As a teacher, you have to believe that no matter your families' race, ethnicity, socioeconomic background and circumstances, home language, and education background, that they can, especially with your willing support, enhance their already existing ability to encourage and foster their children's learning. We believe there are two distinct lenses with which to see our students' families.

NOTE FROM KAREN

How Do We "See" the Families of the Children at Our School?

Dr. Karen Mapp

We suggest this exercise as a way of examining the implicit biases and assumptions you may have about the families at your school. Schools often use a deficit-based lens versus a strength-based lens as it relates to family and communities. For this activity, you will make a list of the positive characteristics that describe your families.

Use the following categories to make a list of the strengths and different types of knowledge and abilities that your families have. Use only asset-based language—do not use any negative phrases or words.

1. Race and ethnic diversity
2. Socioeconomic diversity
3. Occupational diversity
4. Educational diversity

5. Religious diversity
6. Political diversity
7. Talents
8. Other

After creating the lists, answer the following questions:

- Are you utilizing all of the strengths and assets your families have to offer?
- How might you gather information from your families to expand this list?

The Risks of Deficit-Based Thinking

Through the negative lens called "deficit-based thinking" (Valencia, 1997), the world is tinted so that we primarily see problems. We attempt to teach the children "despite their backgrounds," blaming the family or the community or the culture for the challenges the children face. We don't believe that our families have the skills and capacities they need to help their children; rather, we see their lack of education, culture, or English skills as impossible barriers to overcome, and prohibitive of any attempts to cultivate and maintain effective home-school partnerships.

Have you heard any of these statements before?

- "The families are the problem and there is no sense engaging them; they are in the way."
- "Just give me the kids…the families are dysfunctional."
- "Because of their limited education, it doesn't make sense to share data with them; they'll just be overwhelmed."

Unfortunately, we have heard them all. If one believes that students' families and communities are a negative influence on a child's success, it becomes impossible to identify the many ways in which families can meaningfully contribute.

The opinions quoted above are extreme, but deficit-based thinking is not always so overt. As teachers, we should continually question and examine how we understand and see our families. Are we preoccupied with what our students and families don't have—too little money, not enough English? Even if these concerns stem from our caring and concern, the one-dimensional focus on our families' shortfalls can blind us to their strengths.

Seeing our families through this deficit-lens may also make us think that it is our job as teachers to "rescue" or "save" our students from what we regard as awful circumstances, neighborhoods, and families. Resisting the savior mentality—the feeling that we need to rescue our students and their families from themselves—can be difficult. But believing that our students need to be saved from their culture, their communities, or their families runs counter to building relationships with families and respecting the valuable knowledge that they bring to the learning taking place in our classrooms.

NOTE FROM KAREN
A Visit to My Class

Dr. Mapp gives an example of deficit-based thinking.

Dr. Karen Mapp

I had a group of teachers from an innovative school come to my class to talk about their school. When the teachers talked about the core mission of the school, one stated that it was their goal to "inoculate the children from their families and that awful community." My students were horrified. This was a clear example of deficit-mindset and not recognizing the existing positive capacity of the families and community.

Strength-Based Thinking

This brings us to the second of the two lenses, one often referred to as *asset-based* or *strength-based thinking*. Parents have tremendous capacity and knowledge that can contribute to their child's learning and growth. No matter if our families had little formal education, or speak little English, they have a tremendous treasure trove of skills that schools all too often don't acknowledge, respect, or tap.

We offer you the analogy of a tool kit—everyone has a tool kit, but our tools are different. The tools you may have in your kit as a teacher are different from the tools your families possess, but by sharing them we cultivate a wonderful system of support for the children. Seeing the value of everyone's tools—their skills and knowledge—is what it means to have a strength- or asset-based mindset.

We believe this is connected to what Professor Luis Moll at the University of Arizona speaks of as the *funds of knowledge*, the idea that families have explicit and important knowledge about their child and their community that is extremely valuable for a teacher (Moll, Amanti, Neff & González, 2005).

As we mentioned in the Introduction—what your families know contributes to your ability to be the best teacher that you can be and helps to make your job easier. Your families have a trove of information about their child—their learning habits, their interests, the subjects that they enjoy, and even the things that set them off and the things that they don't like—and all of that information is invaluable to you.

Identifying and acknowledging these funds of knowledge that our students' families and communities possess and the myriad ways in which they can positively contribute to their children's education is essential if we want to create strong partnerships. Our families are a part of the solution, not part of the problem, and we practitioners need to see our families as *co-creators* and *co-producers* of the kind of excellent educational opportunities we want for all of our students.

Core Belief 3: Families and school staff are equal partners.

In order to create the best learning experiences for students, we need the knowledge that only families can provide. Seeing families as equal partners and teammates in the work to make sure that all students achieve shapes your approach to family engagement and raises its significance as a part of your practice.

When Karen talks about parents as "equal partners" to practitioners, she often uses the metaphor of an American-style football team. She says:

Dr. Karen Mapp

Even if you are not into football, you might know that the team consists of two parts, the offense and the defense. The offensive part of the team moves the football down the field and scores the touchdowns (the points). The defensive part of a team has the job of stopping the opponent's offense from scoring points.

Imagine if the two parts of the same team didn't respect each other and the skills each brought to the task at hand. Imagine if the offensive team said, "Hey, we do all of the work to score the points! Those guys on the defensive part of the team aren't half as important as we are. No way is their importance equal to ours!"

Is that team going to be successful? Probably not, because the two parts of the same team—a team that has specific goals to meet—don't see themselves as equal partners in the work. Each player on that team, whether he or she is on the offensive or defensive side, has to value the skills and knowledge of every single one of his or her teammates. Even though each member has different skills and a different role to play, all are important to a successful outcome.

Embracing equal partnership as a core belief means that you know that your families have skills, ideas, and knowledge about their children and community that are of value to you. When families see that you value them as members of "the team" of student achievement and development, they will also value your skills and knowledge as their child's teacher.

Kristen Whitaker

A TEACHER'S STORY
Shifting My Core Beliefs

Kristen Whitaker, a high school history teacher at Columbia Heights Education Campus in Washington, DC, tells the story of her shifting beliefs of the power of family engagement. In 2015, she was awarded the National Toyota Family Engagement Teacher of the Year Award.

During my first year of teaching, my principal explained that we would be participating in a school-wide initiative to increase family engagement. We spent all day learning how to properly conduct home visits and engage our families. During this training, I was completely overwhelmed at the thought of having to find time to go to students' homes in addition to all the other teacher responsibilities I was trying to get a handle on. I thought the admin team had some nerve to add more responsibilities on a teacher's already overflowing plate!

As the year began, I came across a student who was more than a handful. You know the type, the one whose reputation precedes them. I could tell he was not a bad kid and wanted to do well, but I was unsure of how I could reach him and have a positive impact on his life. But I knew I had to do something. So, reluctantly, I called his mom and set up a home visit.

The day of the visit came and one of my coworkers and I drove to this student's house. His mother greeted us at the door and, to our very pleasant surprise, she had prepared dinner and laid out a very welcoming experience. Over dinner, I learned a few very important things about my student. I learned that he loved his dog very much (who, by the way, was taller than me!), and he loved to bike around the city and take pictures. I stored this information, as well as so much more, away for use at a later date.

A few days later, that student was very disengaged and a bit combative in class. I told him to take a break from his assignment and come sit with me for a minute. I asked him what he did over the weekend. He replied, "Nothing." I then asked him if he took any cool pictures over the weekend and he instantly perked up. He asked if he could show me, and I told him I would love to see the pictures. Something changed in our relationship at that very moment. He started to see me as someone who actually cared about him and the things he cared about. He knew I was interested in more than just my class content.

Over the next few days, I introduced a project for his class on DC History. Students were required to write about the history of some historical locations around the city. This student was not the least bit interested in completing this project. I thought to myself, "How can I get him to complete his work now that we have established a better relationship?" Then it popped into my head: I would differentiate this assignment for him based upon what I learned about him during the home visit. I told him to take Mojo, his dog, and bike around the city and take pictures of the locations he was originally asked to write about. Then we printed the pictures out, put them on construction paper, and he wrote placards for each of them detailing the history of each location. We BOTH felt so accomplished! He was able to display his pictures and placards like a museum exhibit across the classroom, and because of the home visit, I changed my practice, which resulted in him doing his work and mastering the standards. What a win for us both!

Following this experience, I have become family engagement's biggest cheerleader at my school. I made it my goal to spread the news to all teachers, especially hesitant teachers who did not want to engage the families of their students. I told them it was worth the effort to make these connections. It would improve their instruction as well as the day-to-day success of their students. I began to work as a city-wide teacher trainer for the home-visit project, telling my story to every teacher who would listen.

A PARENT'S STORY

What Teachers Should Know About Parents

Rebecca Brown, a Boston parent, describes the importance of engagement from the families' perspective.

I would really like for teachers to know…we talk about high expectations and we want parents to have high expectations, and I think it would be nice for teachers to know that [they] can teach empowerment to families. I think when [we] families walk in the door, we always have that invisible boundary. As soon as you walk in, "I'm a parent," "I'm a teacher"; we have different roles, but when we talk to each other [about] what's best for the student or the best outcomes…[we unite in our efforts to support our students]. I think if teachers knew how important they are in instilling the idea of high expectations for families, that would be a huge, huge accomplishment.

Core Belief 4: The responsibility for cultivating and sustaining partnerships among school, home, and community rests primarily with school staff, especially school leaders.

In most schools, there exists a hierarchy between school staff and families, which often reflects historical racial, class, and educational hierarchies and divisions. School staff must be willing to reach out and break through existing barriers.

Teachers must understand that they have to be persistent—families will not just greet you with open arms and pile into your classrooms just because you made one call or sent home a nice letter (though such welcoming invitations are important). Building trust takes time and persistence. It may take repeated tries with some families before they understand that you authentically care about their child.

RESEARCH BRIEF

Building Authentic Teacher-Parent Relationships—What It Really Takes

Dr. Soo Hong, Associate Professor of Education at Wellesley College, describes what she's learned from her research on cultivating authentic teacher-parent relationships.

Teachers often work in schools where traditional power dynamics— teachers as experts and families as passive recipients of information— are pervasive. The parent-teacher conference, the bake sales, the fall open house—these practices are ingrained in the life and culture of every school and often perpetuate these unexamined, traditional relationships. In schools that serve marginalized communities, the imbalance of power can be even more severe when educators' beliefs about families are framed by deficit views. Any sensible parent will receive these messages and believe that attempts to engage with the school in productive and meaningful ways are futile.

In a two-year ethnography of five urban teachers, I explored teachers' motivations to engage families fully, and the experiences that led to authentic teacher-parent relationships (Hong, in press). To varying degrees, these teachers came into their practice with an interest in connecting with families and were open-minded about engaging them to support student learning. What they learned, however, was that interest and motivation alone would not facilitate positive working relationships with families.

In their early professional years, these teachers found that many families in marginalized communities carried a history of disrespect and/or trauma from school staff (Hong, in press). As part of this study, I spoke with family members across various school settings to understand how they experienced each teacher's efforts to engage them. Across these conversations, I was struck by the commonplace disrespect parents of color experience in urban schools, particularly but not exclusively by white educators. One mother described her parental responsibility as "protecting" her daughter from the "vicious attacks and accusations and nonstop blaming" she endured in her previous school.

If students and their families experience trauma and violence in schools, it should then come as no surprise that the efforts to engage them require patience, understanding, and the development of trust. With this mindset, teachers in this study believe it is the responsibility of schools to initiate outreach to families. While schools may typically view a lack of parental involvement as indifference or apathy toward their child's education, these teachers have come to understand that when parents are not responsive, it is not because they don't care but because, as one teacher explains, "We have not yet proven that we can be trusted." Invitations to generic family events such as parent-teacher conferences or open houses may be enhanced with communication in different languages or family-friendly event times, but these changes are superficial in an environment where parents do not trust school staff and do not believe that they have their child's best interests in mind. Given the history of disrespect and racial tension that can exist between families and school staff, schools must find ways to develop authentic conversations between school staff and families and design a plan for outreach that reflects an understanding of the diverse families present in the school. It is not an easy journey, but most certainly a rewarding and transformative one.

A TEACHER'S STORY

Trust Me, Family Engagement Is Worth It!

Dwayne Nunez, a 12-year teaching veteran in the Boston Public Schools, discusses how he changed his mind about engaging with families.

Dwayne Nunez

When I began teaching, I was not a believer in the power of home-school partnerships. When I was growing up, my mother wanted me to learn; she read with me and helped me with my homework—but she was never at school except when I was in trouble, which happened a lot! In my experience, most of the time teachers talked to parents because the children were acting up and teachers wanted parents to fix the problem!

As a teacher, I was determined to put my energy into working with my students so they would be successful. I felt like I didn't have the time to work with families and I didn't believe the returns would be worth it. Parents appreciated how much time I put into nurturing their children. However, families didn't carry over the work I was doing with their kids in their homes because I neglected building a relationship with them.

This changed a couple of years ago. I had a parent in my classroom who literally cussed me out whenever I called. I was about to give up, thinking parents just aren't worth it! Instead, I opened myself up to get support from a colleague. We talked about the terrible experiences so many families have had with schools and how for some parents this is going to be the starting point. We practiced together how to be respectful to a parent, even under the most difficult circumstances. Lo and behold, I was able to connect with this parent and she jumped on board. After that, we worked together for the rest of the year and her daughter was transformed.

Another experience that contributed to changing my mind about engaging families is the Special Man Breakfast I organized. Sixty men came together to support the children in their lives. At the end, we had a time for reflection. One granddad stood up and cried. He talked about not being able to be there for his kids because his priorities were work and making money to support the family. Over and over these men were saying, "We want to be here; we just don't know how," or "We have to make money to provide, and we didn't realize how important it was for us to be present." I learned that part of my job as a teacher is to organize opportunities for family members to be able to show their support, to stand up and be counted. As a teacher, you might not believe at first how powerful family engagement can be. What happened to me is that I tried it out, I felt successful, and that made me want to continue. Like me, you might not change your belief until you experience what can happen when you reach out with respect. Trust me, it's worth it!

Ilene Carver

NOTE FROM ILENE

The Power of an Authentic Invitation of Partnership From the Teacher

Ilene remembers a conversation with a parent during her first year of teaching.

This girl's mother said to me, "When you first started calling my home, I did not want to talk with you. I had never had a teacher call my house except to complain about my kids. I have four children," she said, "and on some days I'd get four phone calls from schools telling me how my children were acting up." She went on, "I came to school for that first family presentation because you invited me personally. When I saw my daughter (who was in second grade) standing up reading and speaking before all these families, I was so proud. After that I knew I wanted to come up to school and be a part of things."

Without a doubt, there are obstacles to building relationships with families. We hear from families about their current or past experiences with the schools that they and their children attend or attended. It is clear there is a long history of "us" and "them" relationships between families and schools.

We know from the work of the family engagement Vanderbilt researcher Kathy Hoover-Dempsey (Hoover-Dempsey, Walker & Sandler, 2005) that when parents are invited by school staff, and particularly by you as their child's teacher, it contributes tremendously to the families' sense of being welcomed and honored by the school. And the more personal the invitation, the better; personal phone calls and face-to-face interactions make it clear to families that you sincerely want to partner with them.

Reaching out to families won't always feel immediately comfortable, and, in some cases, it may require perseverance. We believe that whatever you put into the building of relationships with the families of the children in your classrooms and schools will be reaped many times over in both the growth and achievement of your children, and your own sense of increased efficacy and effectiveness as a teacher.

As we mentioned in the Introduction, this kind of work is easiest if you have the backing and support of the school administration. Even if your school leader hasn't made building partnerships with families a top priority, your outreach to families may serve as an important building block to greater family engagement in your whole school. As your colleagues begin to see your success in building meaningful partnerships with families, others may want to join in.

Final Thoughts

In this section we have tried to highlight how your own core beliefs are the foundation of your ability to partner with families and meaningfully engage in this work. If you approach the work with families with a strength-based mindset, you will succeed in your efforts to build positive, meaningful relationships with teachers.

We also wanted to raise the issue and importance of taking some time to interrogate your stereotypes and prejudices. This is particularly important if you come from a racial, ethnic, socioeconomic, or religious background that is different from that of your families. As you likely are aware, in many of our school districts, our students are predominantly from families of color, while the teaching force is predominantly white. A study from the Center for American Progress (2011) found that while students of color make up over 40 percent of students, more than 80 percent of teachers are white.

In her insightful book entitled *"Why Are All the Black Kids Sitting Together in the Cafeteria?": And Other Conversations About Race* (Tatum, 2003), Beverly Tatum pushes all of us, both white educators and educators of color, to examine our beliefs and behaviors and to understand the role they play in our behaviors and actions:

> I assume that we all have prejudices, not because we want them, but simply because we are so continually exposed to misinformation about others. Though I have often heard students or workshop participants describe someone as not having "a prejudiced bone in

his body," I usually suggest that they look again. Prejudice is one of the inescapable consequences of living in a racist society. Cultural racism—the cultural images and messages that affirm the assumed superiority of Whites and the assumed inferiority of people of color—is like smog in the air. Sometimes it is so thick it is visible, other times it is less apparent, but always, day in and day out, we are breathing it in. None of us would introduce ourselves as "smog-breathers" (and most of us don't want to be described as prejudiced), but if we live in a smoggy place, how can we avoid breathing the air?

…Even a member of the stereotyped group may internalize the stereotypical categories about his or her own group to some degree. In fact, this process happens so frequently that it has a name: internalized oppression.

…To say that it is not our fault does not relieve us of responsibility, however. We may not have polluted the air, but we need to take responsibility, along with others, for cleaning it up. Each of us needs to look at our own behavior. Am I perpetuating and reinforcing the negative messages so pervasive in our culture, or am I seeking to challenge them? If I have not been exposed to positive images of marginalized groups, am I seeking them out, expanding my own knowledge base for myself and my children? Am I acknowledging and examining my own prejudices, my own rigid categorizations of others, thereby minimizing the adverse impact they might have on my interactions with those I have categorized? Unless we engage in these and other conscious acts of reflection and reeducation, we easily repeat the process with our children. We teach what we were taught. The unexamined prejudices of the parents are passed on to the children. It is not our fault, but it is our responsibility to interrupt this cycle (pp. 5–7).

While deeply exploring issues of race and cultural consciousness goes beyond the purview of our book, we thought it was critically important and relevant to raise these topics when discussing the examination and development of your core beliefs. We know that you will be more successful at partnering with families if you take the time to explore this challenging but necessary topic more thoroughly, and as such, we have provided you with some additional resources.

Here are a number of books we would suggest you dive into as you begin or continue exploring your core beliefs.

- *Blindspot: Hidden Biases of Good People* (2013) by Mahzarin Banaji
- *Class Matters* (2011) in *The New York Times*
- *Colormute: Race Talk Dilemmas in an American School* (2005) by Mica Pollock
- *Dream Keepers: Successful Teachers of African American Children* (1994) by Gloria Ladson Billings
- *For White Folks Who Teach in the Hood…and the Rest of Ya'll, Too* (2016) by Christopher Emdin
- *Lives in Limbo: Undocumented and Coming of Age in America* (2015) by Roberto Gonzales
- *Mindset: The New Psychology of Success* (2007) by Carol Dweck
- *Rac(e)ing to Class: Confronting Poverty and Race in Schools and Classrooms* (2015) by Richard Milner
- *Respect: An Exploration* (2000) by Sara Lawrence-Lightfoot
- *Unequal Childhoods: Class, Race, and Family Life* (2003) by Annette Lareau
- *We Can't Teach What We Don't Know: White Teachers, Multiracial Schools*, 2nd Edition (2006) by Gary Howard
- *Whistling Vivaldi: How Stereotypes Affect Us and What We Can Do (Issues of Our Time)* (2011) by Claude Steele
- *"Why Are All the Black Kids Sitting Together in the Cafeteria?": And Other Conversations About Race* (2003) by Beverly Tatum

Reflection

- Which of the Four Core Beliefs are most reflected in the work you do with families? Which of the Core Beliefs might you embrace more closely?

- What is your experience with building partnerships with families across race and class?

PARTNERSHIP CLIP

Chapter 1: Your Colleagues Reflect

scholastic.com/PartnerResources

Harness the Power of Partnerships

Powerful partnerships are the foundation of successful family engagement in your classroom and your school. As teachers, we all know that education is a team sport, and the more in sync the team, the better the results. But you might be asking—and rightfully so—what do we mean when we say it is important to build partnerships? What should a true partnership between you and your students' families look like?

While we have examined the mindset you need to engage successfully with families, in this chapter we want to explain our understanding of what great partnerships look and feel like—both at the classroom and the school levels.

First, a quick thought experiment (feel free also to write down or type out your thoughts): Think about someone in your work or at home with whom you enjoy collaborating. This could be a colleague, a friend, a spouse, or even a sibling. Why specifically do you enjoy working with this person? What makes it a productive working relationship? How might you collaborate or share different tasks? How might your strengths and weaknesses complement one another?

Your lists—and the qualities you identified—are the same traits that you can use to help foster effective partnerships with parents, creating working relationships that complement and build on each other, relationships founded on deep-seated trust, where you see each other as equals.

Now, how do we create these partnerships? What do they look like in practice? And what skills and capacities will we need?

Four Types of Partnerships

When Karen L. Mapp and Anne Henderson were discussing the material for their book *Beyond the Bake Sale* (2007), they thought a tool that describes what partnerships between families and schools looked and felt like would be helpful. They aimed to create a tool that would describe what one would see, hear, and experience in schools at various partnership levels. Over the years of their work in the field of family engagement, they had asked practitioners and families questions such as:

- What are school and staff attitudes toward parents and communities?

- Did they hold onto traditional roles and divisions between home and school?

- Had the schools and staff tried to define what family involvement and engagement meant and should mean?

- Had schools actively reached out to community partners?

From these questions and considerations, they developed a rubric outlined in Chapter Two of *Beyond the Bake Sale: The Essential Guide to Family-School Partnerships* to describe four categories of schools to understand how welcoming and active they are in partnering with families (Henderson et al., 2007). They described the four school levels as:

- Partnership School

- Open-Door School

- Come-If-We-Call School

- Fortress School

Below, we describe in more detail what kinds of approaches and attitudes you might see in each type of school.

Fortress School (Below Basic)

At Fortress Schools, engaging with families is a low priority and isn't thought of as being connected to student outcomes. The standard events for families are held each year mostly out of compliance. Staff have experienced very low turnout at most events and, as a result, are discouraged and not enthusiastic about family engagement.

Here's what you might hear and experience at a Fortress School:

- "Parents don't care about their children's education, and they are the primary reason that the students are failing."

- "Parents don't come to conferences, no matter what we do. We send notices home, provide food and childcare at events, and they still don't come. It's just more proof that our families don't value education."

- Principal selects a small group of "cooperative parents" to help out and serve on the decision-making committees that require parent participation. These chosen parents don't necessarily reflect the diversity of the families who send their children to the school.

- Teachers feel that family engagement should be left to the guidance staff or a parent coordinator as teachers need to focus on their realm, teaching and learning.

- "Information about the curriculum, standards, and learning goals is way too advanced for the parents at our school. Some don't speak English, some never graduated from high school. We don't want to overwhelm them with information that they just won't understand."

- "We don't think it's appropriate for families to visit our classrooms— we don't want them spying on us or critiquing our teaching."

Come-If-We-Call School (Basic)

Come-If-We-Call Schools are more positive about the concept of engaging with families, but the school sets the terms of engagement. Most of the communication is one way—from the school to home, and families can come to the school only when invited. These schools operate with a "don't call us, we'll call you" culture.

Here's what you might hear and experience at a Come-If-We-Call School:

- Families are invited to the fall open house or back-to-school night to hear the school and classroom rules and regulations.
- All contact with teachers and school leaders must go through front office staff; teachers never share their contact information with families.
- Workshops for families are planned by school staff without parent input or feedback.
- Families can visit school on designated days such as report card pickup day.
- Parents call the office to retrieve teacher-recorded messages about homework.

Open-Door School (Proficient)

Open-Door Schools make family engagement a priority and see it as an important part of student success. More targeted efforts are made to reach out to and invite families to be engaged with a focus on helping families to support their children's learning.

Here's what you might hear and experience at an Open-Door School:

- Family engagement is coordinated by a committee or an "Action Team" that includes families and school staff.
- Parent-teacher or parent-student-teacher conferences are held at least twice a year.
- The school holds various events for families, such as literacy nights, math nights, or science fairs, three or four times a year.
- Parents can raise issues at PTA/PTO or site council meetings or see the principal.
- An "open door" policy and protocol exists at the school: Families are welcomed to visit the school.
- Family diversity is recognized through multicultural events and translation is provided at these and other events held at the school.

Partnership School (Advanced)

You might be saying, "The Open-Door School sounds pretty good; what needs to be added for it to become a Partnership School?" At a Partnership school, family engagement isn't done out of compliance or because of mandates. Engaging with families is seen as a commitment and a key component of the school's functioning. Families are seen as true partners in the teaching and learning process and are valued as knowledgeable and important contributors to school and student improvement.

Here's what you might hear and experience at a Partnership School:

- Families are regarded as full partners with school staff in improving educational outcomes.

- All family events and initiative activities are connected to student learning and development.

- Families and school staff have developed a clear, open process for resolving problems.

- Parent-to-parent networks are valued and cultivated.

- Families are actively involved in decisions on school improvement.

- Staff are intentional about developing relationships of trust and respect with all families and engage in relationship-building practices such as home visits.

- "We're ALL family here at this school: our students, our staff, our families."

Where might your school fall on this list? We imagine that some of the bullets from each list will resonate with you. *Beyond the Bake Sale* provides a detailed and expanded checklist to determine where your school falls on this continuum.

Strong partnerships may start at any one of these four levels. True, it will be much easier to build vibrant working relationships with families if you work in a Partnership School, but even if you work in a school you believe is a Fortress School, you can still create great opportunities to connect with families.

Your honest and committed work with parents might be just the catalyst you need to help transform your entire school into a space that is more welcoming and committed to working with families.

PARTNERSHIP CLIP
Understanding Dual Capacity-Building Framework

scholastic.com/PartnerResources

Conditions for Effective Partnerships

You might be feeling unprepared to build these partnerships. We suspect that you've never received extensive training in how to engage families. Many teachers say that the extent of their training on family engagement was a workshop or single course session on parent-teacher conferences. You are not alone. In one U.S.-based 2009 survey (Markow & Pieters, 2009), teachers and principals identified family engagement as the most challenging component of their responsibilities. Yet, traditionally and unfortunately, the educational community has not effectively built the skills and capacities of teachers and other school staff to create meaningful partnerships with families. While schools and teacher training programs often offer myriad professional development programs and courses around the nuances of curriculum development or behavior management, too few are dedicated to meaningful training for the essential work of effective family engagement.

Families, too, may feel unprepared to be powerful partners. They might face cultural or structural barriers that make it hard to connect with teachers and schools. They might find it challenging or intimidating to navigate our complex educational system, or they might feel unwelcome or not trusted in our school halls and classrooms.

Here's the challenge: Even though many teachers and other school staff express a strong desire to forge stronger partnerships with families, many tell us that, quite frankly, they don't know how. No one has ever shared with them what effective practice in this area actually looks like.

This limited capacity on the part of school staff and families served as the impetus for the development of the United States Department of Education (USDOE) Dual Capacity Framework for Family-School Partnership. Karen and the USDOE collaborated to create the framework, and a publication entitled "Partners in Education" was authored by Karen L. Mapp and Paul Kuttner describing the framework (Mapp & Kuttner, 2014). This research-based framework was designed to provide you and your schools with guidance on how to plan successful family engagement events, programs, and initiatives (for more information on and a diagram of the Dual Capacity Framework for Family-School Partnerships, see http://www.sedl.org/pubs/framework/).

The Dual Capacity Framework identifies five *process conditions* that align quite nicely with the practices we've seen in action at Partnership Schools. These conditions help set the stage for the information, recommendations, and advice we will share with you in the upcoming chapters.

The Five Process Conditions

The *Merriam-Webster Dictionary* defines the word *process* as "a series of actions that produce something or that lead to a particular result." As such, the process conditions articulate what we now know about the actions or steps we need to build into our planning of a family engagement event, program, or initiative to ensure its success.

Linked to Learning

The first process condition is that whatever we plan for and with families should be *linked to learning*—in other words, aligned with the learning and developmental goals for the students. Ask yourself the following questions: "Do my families leave the events at our school or in my classroom knowing more about what their children should know and be able to do? Did we provide an opportunity for our families to learn and master a new skill in support of a particular learning goal?" If your answers are "no" to these questions, you are not alone! It's pretty common that many of the traditional family events and initiatives that take place in schools and in classrooms are out of alignment with the teaching and learning goals of the school.

Relational

Our efforts must be intentional about building relationships of trust and respect with families. Families and school staff have to be given an opportunity to learn about each other, to share stories, and to build partnerships that are based on respect. We can't emphasize this enough—without a strong foundation of trust and respect, it is next to impossible to create strong partnerships.

Developmental

The third condition actually speaks to the tenor and tone of attempts to build partnerships with families. When your family engagement practice is developmental, it assumes that families already have strengths and knowledge on which you can build (as opposed to regarding families as empty or damaged vessels in need of services and "fixing"). For many of us who work in communities confronted with the challenges of poverty and adverse conditions, it may be hard, at times, not to regard families through a deficit-based lens. In so doing, we may overlook the fact that those families have knowledge and skills that can help us develop and grow as practitioners.

Collaborative

Initiatives should strive to bring families and staff together so that they can learn from and with each other. By collaborative, we mean that this relationship between families and practitioners is reciprocal and builds on the strengths of both parties. Everyone is viewed through an asset-based lens—teachers, families, community members, and the students. Under collaborative process conditions, everyone is listened to, contributes, and is empowered. This condition means that initiatives must be designed where true sharing among staff and families is valued and cultivated.

A Turning Point for Michael:
A Collaborative Family Conference

Ilene Carver

Ilene discusses the impact of home-school partnership on another student, Michael.

For the first six weeks of second grade, Michael rarely participated in class. He almost always sat away from where instruction was taking place, often hanging upside down with his feet dangling in the air. Day after day, he spent his time inwardly focused without regard to the 21 other children, the teachers, or the learning routines of the classroom. The family conference was a turning point. We sat together: Mom, Dad, Michael, and his teachers. Michael declared, "I want to learn second-grade math, and I want to learn how to pay attention for instruction." Mom, Dad, and I made a mutual commitment to stay in touch about Michael's progress, and to work together to provide him with the support he needed to be successful in the classroom. Since then, Michael began meeting daily in a small math group within the classroom, took part in a guided reading group, engaged in writing tasks and science exploration, and generally participated in the learning activities of our classroom. Not only did he make significant growth in math and other subjects we were studying, he also sat right-side up, like the other children, in the area where instruction takes place. Frequent texts back and forth between home and school made clear that we were all on the same team and high expectations were continuous. While Michael's focus still wandered at times, his progress was immense. This 180-degree turnaround could not and would not have happened without the united efforts that grew out of that family-school partnership.

Interactive

We adults learn by doing. In fact, active learning is even more important for adults than for children! To master any skill, we all need a chance to practice it; thus, our family engagement events should be interactive (and fun!). We sometimes have a tendency to hand our families lists of activities and instructions of things to do at home to support their children's learning, but with no opportunity to practice, get support, and discuss the activities, families are often confused about what to do.

PARTNERSHIP CLIP

Linking Family Engagement to Learning

scholastic.com/PartnerResources

RESEARCH BRIEF

Principles of Adult Learning

Here's what we know from research about the ways that adults learn best:

1. **Adults must want to learn.** (Helping their children is a strong motivator for learners who are parents.)
2. **Adults will learn only what they feel they need to learn.**
3. **Adults learn by doing.**
4. **Adult learning focuses on problems, and the problems must be realistic.**
5. **Experience affects adult learning.**
6. **Adults learn best in an informal situation.**
7. **Adults want guidance.**

For more on the topic of adult learning, check out this website: www.literacy.ca/professionals/professional-development-2/principles-of-adult-learning.

Final Thoughts

We offer you these frameworks, conditions, and rubrics as a starting place for you to assess where your school stands and where you should start on this journey. As you read further, you will notice that throughout this book we will offer examples of initiatives, programs, examples of practice, and suggestions that mirror the conditions outlined above. We know that not every practice you put in place will have all the conditions down pat, but we offer this as a guide for your future work.

PARTNERSHIP CLIP
Chapter 2:
Your Colleagues Reflect

Listen to your colleagues reflect on their experiences with family engagment.

scholastic.com/PartnerResources

You may be thinking, "Oh my gosh! This seems like a lot! How can I ever move my classroom and my school to a robust partnership school?" This process will take time and hard work—but wherever you are, whatever level your school has achieved, you can make a difference. In the words of our friend and colleague Michele Brooks, former Assistant Superintendent for Family and Student Engagement in Boston: "Where you are is where you start and where you start is a good place…because you are starting."

Reflection

Describe where you and your school are on the path to effective family-school partnerships. Use the Fortress through Partnership School descriptions to support your discussion.

Welcome, Honor, and Connect With Your Families

The school year is fast approaching; it is time to put your hopes for family engagement into action. When should you reach out? How should you reach out? What should you say when you have your first face-to-face meeting with your students' families or meet them for the first time on the other end of a phone line? In this chapter, we hope to walk you through the first few months of school and help guide your thinking and practice as you build powerful partnerships.

Getting Started: The Joining Process

In her research about why and how families are engaged in education, Karen heard from families that when school staff welcomed their participation in their children's education, honored families' unique contributions and engagement styles, and connected families to their children's learning, families felt empowered to be engaged in their children's education and excited about building partnerships with school staff. These three components make up the Joining Process (Mapp, 2003), which provides you with an outline of the strategies you can employ to get off to a great start with your families.

Welcoming

Your initial conversations and interactions with families are critical for setting the tone of your relationship for the entire school year. Just as you put a lot of thought and planning into setting up your classroom and your curriculum, we suggest this same intentionality and forethought is important to build your partnerships with families. Families need to know and trust that you fully embrace and invite their engagement. Being intentional and thoughtful about how you welcome, express, and demonstrate your desire to work with families is key. Welcoming families from the start and asserting the desire for two-way communication is very important.

PARTNERSHIP CLIP

Engaging in the Joining Process

scholastic.com/PartnerResources

By reaching out to families *before* you've even met the students, they will see that your intent is to build an important relationship with them, not just with their child. In addition, you will gain information from the families that will enable you to plan the best teaching and learning strategies for their child.

As we pointed out in Chapter 1, you may encounter barriers created by decades of negative interactions between schools and families. It is quite possible that parents will be wary and untrusting when you first reach out. Don't despair! By being consistent with your message to families that you want, cherish, and expect their engagement, you will over time build their trust and cultivate a two-way respectful partnership. We also pointed out in Chapter 1 that your own core belief in this type of partnership will be key in your ability to convey to families that you value their engagement.

Honoring

Making it clear to families through your words and actions that their knowledge of their child is very important to you honors families' funds of knowledge (Moll et al., 2005). For example, stating to families, "You are your child's first teacher, and I'm interested in learning from you about your child" signifies to them that you value their knowledge and consider them experts. This begins the process of building a trusting and respectful relationship right from the start.

In contrast, if the first time you contact a parent is to give them bad news about their child's behavior or academic performance, your chance of building an effective relationship with that family is much more difficult, if not impossible. We are sure that you have experienced a circumstance where an exchange with someone you met for the first time started off on the wrong foot. It's often much harder to build a positive relationship with someone when that happens. We strongly recommend that you avoid this at all costs and spend some intentional time before the school year starts connecting in positive ways with your families. Teachers have told us that by doing this important work early on, future conversations about challenging topics go smoothly and are resolved quickly.

Connecting

In the Dual Capacity-Building Framework, linking our family engagement initiatives to learning was a key *process* condition. Connecting families to the learning that takes place in the classroom is an important condition of building partnership. Parents *want* to understand what it is their child will be learning in the coming year and will look to you to share information and advice on how to partner to ensure their child's success.

Foundational Strategies

Before school starts, as you plan for a new school year, here are three important foundational strategies we have found for connecting with families. We see these strategies as the cornerstones for building an effective family-school partnership early on.

- The First Contact: Welcome Phone Calls
- Home Visits
- The Back-to-School Night or Open House

On the following pages, we will dive into each strategy in depth. We know each of these can be challenging and perhaps even intimidating, not least because you will likely have a large number of children in your class. We hope to help you think about how you approach each strategy, focusing on understanding the best outcomes and then creating a plan for how to make it happen. We also have included some ideas for activities and protocols you might want to incorporate into your plan.

We know that these strategies may be tricky and difficult for the middle and high school teachers reading this book. We realize that you have many more students, sometimes as many as 150 or more, and so practices used at the elementary school level might not work for you. We will provide alternative strategies and suggestions for you within each of these that come from the middle and secondary school teachers with whom we spoke as part of our research for this book. Some of the suggestions may mean that you partner with other teachers or school staff to carry out the initiative.

The First Contact: Welcome Phone Calls

The beginning of the school year is three weeks away, you are knee-deep in curriculum maps and decorating (or redecorating) your classroom. It's time to begin reaching out to your new partners: your students' families.

As we mentioned, your first contact sets a powerful and lasting welcoming tone that encourages parents to engage with you. Investing early—putting the extra time, thought, and energy into reaching out—will give you the best shot at fostering the strong relationships with families that can help transform your classroom.

We suggest two key ways of building that initial relationship, ideally even before the school year has begun: 1) welcome phone calls and 2) home visits.

Welcoming Phone Calls to Families

Phone calls home have unfortunately developed a very bad reputation. They are for "reporting something bad" that happened in the classroom.

As teachers, we have a great opportunity to set the tone for our phone calls right at the beginning of the year, demonstrating our commitment to engaging parents on much more than just "discipline." An easy first step is to plan early: Reach out to your school and see if you can get families' contact information as soon as possible. While getting the correct numbers may take some time, we recommend that you reach out to your families before school begins or within the first three weeks of the start of school.

Once you have your parents' phone numbers, what are you going to say when they pick up the phone? You might feel anxious, which we totally understand. Some traditional conversations might focus on providing parents with a list of school calendar reminders and tips for the first week of school. Yet we suggest you hold off on these for a moment. This first phone call, somewhat like a first date, is about making a good first impression.

A note for high school teachers: We realize that if you are teaching at a traditional high school, you might have as many as 150 students—very different from the 20–30 you might have if you are a primary teacher in the lower grades. You might be asking: How will I call all 150 before the school year?! Our suggestion, and the suggestion of a number of high school teachers we spoke with, is to start with your advisory students or homeroom students.

NOTE FROM JESSICA

The Shock of a Good News Phone Call!

Jessica Lander

Jessica shares the story of when she called the mother of one of her students to tell her about something great about her child.

I still remember the first time I called home simply to share something special a student, John, had done. John's mom was shocked—she had never received a call to tell her about something good her son had done, only when he was in trouble! By the end of the year, our biweekly phone conversations often stretched a half-hour or more and covered a range of topics—from John's work in my class, to his other classes, and also afterschool activities.

Before school begins, we hope you can structure time to call these 15–25 students. Then, as the year progresses, one strategy we've heard is to divide the rest of your 100–125 students into groups (perhaps by class) and try to call each group over the course of a two-week period.

We hope that this phone call will be the start of many to come, and that you see it as the beginning of your relationship and partnership with families. This phone call is a chance to put your core beliefs into action!

Convey to your families that you want to work with them as partners in order to best support their child. Honoring and acknowledging parents as their child's first teachers will send a clear message that you hope to both learn from them and work with them throughout the year.

Sonya Brown

A TEACHER'S STORY
Making the Call to Families

Boston high school teacher Sonya Brown describes how she makes her first phone calls to families at the beginning of the year.

I come from the generation where people like to hear each other's voices over the phone. I like to introduce myself at the beginning of the semester to the families of the students in my courses. I tell them what our course is about and give my contact information. I say, "Please feel free to contact me anytime you have a question, concerns, or want to share anything that you think would help your child engage better in class." Having that kind of first contact helps families to know that they can reach out to you. Some families want to do that and some not at all. It's important that the initial contact is positive because later you may have to tell families their child is struggling. If you've had a positive initial contact, families are much more likely to understand that you are their ally and want to do everything possible to make sure each child does well.

A PARENT'S STORY

Receiving the Call From a Teacher

Parent Jamila Nichols describes her reaction to getting a phone call from her child's teacher at the beginning of the school year.

Jamila Nichols

When she called me before school even began, that mattered to me. It let me know that she is interested in getting to know not just my child but me as well. It helped me to know that she recognized that my knowledge of my child is important.

Strategies for Partnering With Families Who Are Learning English

Phone calls to the homes of your students will help you identify who among your families speaks different languages and whom you will need support in communicating with. For these families, you will need to find a translator (likely someone in your school community) to help you with future communication. We suggest taking the time to learn a few phrases in the major languages your families might speak. Learning phrases such as "Hello, I'm your child's teacher. I will call back with someone who speaks [fill in home language]" can go a long way in establishing partnerships with your families.

Sabine Ferdinand

Some Advice About Phone Numbers

We know that some teachers might feel uncomfortable giving out their personal phone number to families. Sabine Ferdinand, a fourth-year teacher in Boston teaching first and second grades, has this to say about sharing phone numbers with families.

Between face-to-face conferences, I maintain relationships with families primarily by phone. I give out my phone number before school starts and my families not only appreciate it, but have all been respectful of me and my time. In my four years as a teacher, I haven't felt the need to set limits. This is due to the fact that we have an unspoken agreement that we don't call each other at times that would disturb our lives. On a practical level, there are times where either my families or I need to communicate urgent messages with one another, so sending out a text is quick and effective. More important, I think that giving out my phone number sends a message that I think about your child beyond school hours and I know you want to think about learning beyond the school day.

Home Visits

Home visits and face-to-face meetings at community events are an incredibly powerful and meaningful way to reach out to families, particularly right at the beginning of the year. Stepping outside of the school grounds, going to parents instead of asking them to come to you, and making the effort to visit in their neighborhood and home are all powerful signals that you are invested in building this important relationship.

Home visits are naturally more complicated and require more planning than phone calls, but can be extremely powerful. We realize, too, that suggesting that you conduct home visits may seem excessive and possibly downright scary. The home visits that we are suggesting are not designed to assess or evaluate your families; rather, the aim is to build relationships of trust and respect with families, factors that are key to your eventual partnership with them.

Rather than doing this on your own, we suggest that your school look into and discuss the adoption of home visits as a school-family engagement initiative. We recommend that you contact other schools that have conducted these relational home visits or the Parent Teacher Home Visits organization (www.pthvp.org) based in Sacramento, California, to get advice and training prior to conducting your own home visits.

The Parent Teacher Home Visits website presents a list of five non-negotiables for family home visits, which we believe are a great starting place for you to do this work successfully:

1. Visits are always voluntary for educators and families, and arranged in advance.

2. Focus of the first visit is relationship-building; we discuss hopes and dreams.

3. Teachers are trained and compensated for visits outside their school day.

4. No targeting—visit all or a cross section of students.

5. Educators conduct visits in pairs, with reflection on assumptions, strengths, and bringing what they learned back to the classroom.

We realize that you might have some initial concerns about conducting home visits not just limited to figuring out how to start a successful conversation. You might be asking yourself, is home visiting safe? What if I see signs of abuse or neglect? Carrie Rose, executive director of Parent Teacher Home Visits, addresses some of the most common concerns she has heard over many years of successfully doing this work:

Reflections From Carrie Rose, Parent Teacher Home Visits

Carrie Rose

1 **Staff safety concerns:** Everyone is worried about safety and liability. During our training, we share that PTHV has operated continuously in schools since 1998. We've scaled up to hundreds of schools in 19 different states. PTHV does tens of thousands of home visits across the country every year. Never once in all these years have we had a person harmed in the course of our visits. There are three reasons why this is true. First, the visits are voluntary for everyone and arranged in advance. Second, we send folks out in teams of two. Third, we role-play out questions or concerns so staff feel equipped to take care of themselves or their partners if something should arise. Well-planned, purposeful partnering (both in preparation and in debriefing after visits), not only ensures safety, it reflects the collaborative structure of the PTHV model.

2 **Mandated reporting concerns:** This is another common concern for schools and districts, given that staff are mandated reporters. During the training we share that this is statistically very unlikely to happen to visitors under our model because a) the family agreed to the visit; b) you called to remind them you were coming the day before or the day of the visit and they did not cancel; c) you showed up when you said you would be there; and d) when you did arrive at the home, the family member let you in the door. So, with multiple chances to decline the visit, reportable situations are unlikely. It is our belief that if in the VERY rare event a family admits an educator into a reportable situation, they are asking for help. Again, we role-play concerns folks might have and review the site protocol for a possible report because, statistically speaking, this is much more likely to happen at the school than on one of our home visits.

3 **Is secondary school adaptation of this model really possible?** It is not only possible, high schools do some of the best home visiting around the country! There are, however, logistical challenges that are not present at the elementary grade levels that must be addressed. For smaller high schools, staff tend to use small learning communities or other natural infrastructure to set a ratio of 20 students to one teacher for visits. In our larger comprehensive high schools, our partners adopted our model so that the first visit is a transitional visit as the student is coming into 9th grade, and the second visit is a career- or college-readiness visit in 11th or 12th grade. These visits are effective and powerful for students, families, and staff, and challenge beliefs about the difficulty of engaging families at the secondary school level.

When it comes to the actual launch and sustainability of home visiting, our experience is that the real barriers are a) time (everyone is busy) and b) fears, usually connected to unexamined bias and assumptions, often based on race, ethnicity, socioeconomic status, gender, and the like. We spend time on these as well during our training. In addition, parent testimonies in our trainings are powerful opportunities to shift perspective and ease possible fears of educators.

Addressing barriers and assumptions is not only essential to our training, but also an essential part of our transformative model. At the end of each home visit, the staff reflect on these questions:

1. What did I think was going to be true about the family?

2. What strength does the student or family have that I did not know about before this visit?

3. How am I going to shift my work back in the classroom to leverage this knowledge/asset?

Once educators begin the process of visiting and reflecting, their fears dissipate and they reap the rewards of their time investment.

A PRACTITIONER'S STORY

Flipping the Power Dynamic Through Home Visits

Elizabeth Canada

Elizabeth Canada, a former teacher and Family Engagement Coach, describes the power in going to parents instead of asking them to come to you.

Oftentimes, we, as educators, ask the families to come to our kingdom: the classroom. We want them to cross our threshold and come to a place where we feel comfortable. When I had my own classroom, I thought of any outsider—including other teachers—as just that: outsiders. The classroom was my space, with my decorations of postcards and a solid mixture of organization and disorganization. I was in control of my space.

But the home visit flips that power dynamic. We visit with families where they feel most comfortable; this may be in their home, or it could be in a public place, like their child's soccer practice, a library, or a coffee shop. Teachers have told me that some parents asked them to conduct the home visit at their workplace, which is essentially the opposite of a parent event at a school! I tell my teachers that a home visit can be anywhere that is not on school grounds; go out and meet with the family in their space.

The transformation after a visit is virtually immediate. The educators leave changed. The family comes away changed. The student will remember this experience for months, perhaps years. A teacher recently told me that every single day—EVERY day!— a student she visited asks her, "Do you remember when you came to my house?" The home visit was seven months ago.

The goal of the home visit is to learn more about the family (parents, grandparents, cousins—everyone is welcome!), to authentically listen and learn because we care about the family and the students as people first. Asking a mom what her hopes and dreams are for her child can sometimes render her speechless—perhaps no one has asked her that before. Even more likely? No one from a school has asked her that. But let me tell you: She has hopes and dreams for her child. Every family does. The home visit provides us with insight into what those hopes and dreams are, and how we can be the best educators for the students when they are in our classrooms.

Before you set up home visits, check with your school to see if they have a program already in place to support teachers to conduct such visits, or if they partner with a nonprofit that does trainings on how best to approach incorporating home visits into your practice.

Best practice suggests that you conduct home visits with another teacher or staff member. You don't want to be hampered by pens and pencils and be busily scribbling while trying to talk with and, more important, listening to parents. Going with another person allows you to notice and remember different things and also gives you a partner to review what you want to remember once the visit has been completed. A potential partner for home visits could be a teacher who will have your students next year.

Naturally, it is incredibly important to call families first and arrange a time that is convenient to them. You should never show up on their doorstep unannounced. Remember, too, that not all families will be comfortable at first inviting you into their homes. You don't necessarily need to meet families in their home.

Strategies for Partnering With Families Who Are Learning English

As Carrie Rose strongly encourages, you should always conduct home visits in pairs. She has found in her many years of experience that there are almost always members of the school community who speak the languages of the school's families—these might not be other teachers, but school nurses, librarians, lunch staff, custodial workers, etc. In some cases, there might also be parents who would be willing to come with you to help translate. We stress, though, that students should not be put in the role of translating for you and their families.

If they express some discomfort with a home visit, in your conversation with them, ask about other places in their community where they will feel most comfortable: a local coffee shop, a community center, a library. The important part is that you are going to them, not having them come to you.

A TEACHER'S STORY

How Home Visits Changed Me

Melissa Bryant

Home visits are not just impactful for parents. Melissa Bryant, a former third- and fourth-grade teacher, and current Director of Culture at Stanton Elementary in Washington, DC, describes how home visits helped transform how she saw her community.

I think family engagement has helped me, even outside of being a teacher, become a better person. I used to be super judgmental and put parents in boxes.

For example: I would meet you (the parent) and if I had to call you and say, "Johnny threw a book," and you don't have a working phone, I'm already judging you. And if I call you and you are acting like it's my fault that Johnny threw the book and you're yelling at me, then automatically I put you in Box 1: You don't care. And I don't work as hard for you because you don't really care about your kid or how he learns.

And then there is Box 2: So Johnny threw a book; I call you. Now every time I call you, you answer, but Johnny keeps doing the same thing over and over and over. So it seems as though you care: You pick up my phone calls and attempt to control Johnny, but then he's not changing. So I'm judging: "You need to do more with your kid, so your kid can learn." So that's Box 2.

And then there's the good box, Box 3. So Johnny throws a book and I call you and you promise: "I'm going to get on him. I'm going to get on him—he doesn't get any Nintendo." Then I think, "Oh, this parent really cares. I like this parent. I'm going to work harder for this parent."

So before I learned to do real family engagement, I would automatically assume that there are parents who care about their kids, and parents who don't. But I learned that every parent cares about his or her kids. Every parent wants their kid to be great. Nobody sends their kid to school and says, "You should throw a book at your teacher, 'cause that is exactly how I send you to school to act." Nobody does that, so I think, through family engagement, I've just become less judgmental. Like they don't have a working number? Let me ask the family if there is a number at which I can reach them. Their child is having a problem at school? The parents are probably having the same problem at home; let me see if I can help arrange for some support for the family through community partners, tutoring, or mental health services.

There is no judging, because I know you now. I've been to your house, I've sat with you, I've done a home visit with you. I already know you care about your kids. I think everything I do now is from the mindset that everybody cares and everybody is trying to be helpful.

A TEACHER'S STORY
Bringing the Heart From Home to School

Meg Bruton, a veteran 25-year kindergarten teacher (and indeed, Jessica's kindergarten teacher), speaks to the importance of home visits conducted before the start of school for a teacher's success with students throughout the year.

Meg Bruton

Each summer, I'd begin planning early for the imminent kindergarten school year, getting the classroom ready, painting furniture, ordering supplies, recalibrating summer clock to fall clock, catching up on colleagues' lives, and the like. Similar to most teachers of any age, I'd feel those familiar twinges of both anticipation and anxiety in those late days of summer. Yet nothing became more important in that preparation than the home visits I conducted before the beginning of the year. These visits, which seemed daunting the first time I did them, were often met with a bit of nervousness on my part, yet they heralded what would become the first block in the foundational relationship I hoped to cultivate with each student's family, and with the students themselves. These visits not only helped me grow as a teacher, but they allowed me to expand my understanding and definition of family, parenting, and the diversity found inside those constructs. They began crucial dialogue patterns necessary when two different caretaking units, the teacher and family, set out to create a trusting and mutual learning atmosphere and road map for not only the student, but for me and the family. Building authentic relationships took time, and "turf" mattered. If my students and families felt out of their comfort zones at school, then I could leave my own comfort zone to meet them in theirs.

These visits were successful if we carefully planned beforehand. Before GPS technology, we used printed maps to plot out the best ways to geographically chunk visits together. Then we'd send our visitation schedule to families—and we'd be off—not unlike a "Teachers' Road Trip" adventure. Letting families know what to expect ahead of time was important. What was the purpose of the trip? What were the expectations? How long would it be? Could siblings be there? I'd let families know that it was a short and informal visit so their child could meet us in the comfortable space of the home and nothing out of the ordinary needed to happen. The child might like to show us a few special things, for example, the child's bedroom. I'd provide a few sample questions—and answers—the child might have for us about the new school year and our classroom. I'd bring photos of the class pet. Share the pillow fabric for the pillow each child received at school. We'd take a photo of the child, which we'd put in the child's cubby to greet him or her on their first day.

Upon arrival, we were usually met by nervous families or parents and a nervous child. This first meeting might be a little awkward or forced, but once the child became the focus, showing us something unique such as a favorite cuddly stuffed animal, everything became more relaxed. Of course, no matter how much planning went into the visits, they always surprised me. I could never have planned for the visit into the apartment of a young Haitian child who met me in a vibrant pink party dress with a dozen ribbons in her hair, smiling from ear-to-ear as she offered me tiny tea sandwiches her mother had made for me. How moved I'd feel when on that same visit, her father, beaming, pulled down the family bible to show me many of his ancestors who attended grade school in Port-Au-Prince; how he said of his daughter, standing by his side, "She will surprise you!" I remember getting lost in winding city streets to reach the home of a child I was told came from a very strict, traditional family. Both parents were very important lawyers in the city. How unexpected to be met at the door with everyone in their pajamas! The family seemed to be in a fit of giggles during the entire visit. Yet, on the first day of school, the child was incredibly focused and serious. Wow. How lucky to get a glimpse into this other world of the child!

The home visit served many purposes. It eased the transition the student and family would have coming into a new environment. Many of these students had spent their first few years in a family day care or preschool before even entering kindergarten with me. For most, the BIG elementary school would be a significant adjustment. It showed the students that the adults had a desire, a willingness, to know each other on their behalf. The visits also would make it easier to deliver news that might be challenging to hear as a parent. Brainstorming together would be necessary for a child's school experience to be much more successful. This point was never clearer than when I had a young student who began exhibiting incredible stress and aggression after the initial first month of school. His mom had shared at the home visit, "We are so excited for him to start school, but we're a little nervous about his behavior at times. I hope you'll let us know if you notice things." This eagerness to partner with me became an important step in getting this student a proper evaluation and a solid plan for the year as we continued to define supports he needed for a successful year. He had been calm and happy on his home visit, so I knew this child could thrive if the right adaptations were put in place for him. Having these multiple perspectives deepened my understanding of both the child and the family. How ironic that one of my tasks as a teacher would be to help open children up to multiple perspectives in their worlds.

After these summertime visits, my own anxiety about this largely unknown group lessened considerably! I had context for these kids, had a sense of what their mornings were like, where they came from. I had met the families and guardians of the children we would have in common for the year. I had been on "their turf" and now they were coming to "mine," and we would make it "ours" over the course of the long year together.

It was never lost on me how when I entered the child's home, the parents got to be in the role of expert of their child. They brought so much to the table in my understanding of the child as a learner and social being. I needed them.

Final Thoughts About Home Visits

We realize that the concept of home visits might be a heavy lift for your school and for your community. A common barrier to a home-visit initiative is finding the funding to compensate you and other members of your school community who participate in visits. We know from our experience that they are outstanding contributors to powerful home-school partnerships, and we encourage you to at least investigate the possibility of conducting this kind of practice at your school. One possible source of funding if you are a Title I school is the family engagement allocation that is designated for your school.

We know that families often have a long and not-so-positive home/school partnership history and less-than-effective relationships with the school community. Thoughtful home visits can begin to help you chart a new path for family partnerships. What makes these visits so successful is that you are meeting families where they are. Meeting families in their home or in their community signifies that you are willing to go the extra mile (quite literally) to meet with your families and build partnerships.

An Invitation Into the Classroom: Back-to-School Night and Open House

You've successfully gotten through the first month of school. You've finally learned all your students' names and are starting to learn about each individual child's quirks and interests. You've laid out your class expectations and, with any luck, the days are starting to fall into a semblance of routine. Now comes your school's Back-to-School Night or Open House event!

Traditionally, these events are structured in such a way that families are *talked at*—usually by the school leader and the teacher. These become occasions for the schools to lay down the law and describe the rules of the school and classroom. We encourage you to restructure these events to be more family-focused, to create time and space for families to network with each other and for families and staff to get to know each other. Make your Back-to-School/Open House event an opportunity to honor your families and make sure you hear and value their unique voices. This is an important opportunity to experience and realize the classroom as a learning community that includes the students, families, and you, the teacher. When Karen travels throughout the country and asks school staff why they do these events the same way every year, their response is often, "That's the way we've always done it." Sound familiar?

There is no policy written anywhere that says Back-to-School Nights have to be done the same predictable way. We encourage you to break the mold! Be creative—even if only in your own classroom! Back-to-School/Open House events are great opportunities to gather your learning community of families and students together.

Such events are not just about deepening the connection between you and families, but also about families and their children connecting over their learning in your classroom. Your families' contributions should be seen as integral to the overall teaching, learning, and expectations for the school year. Student success may depend on the extent to which teachers and families are partnering effectively.

Additionally, it can be a great time and space to help parents connect with other parents. Particularly in schools where students may come from communities up to 30 minutes away, families likely will not know each other initially outside of the school. We hope you come to see these beginning-of-the-year events as a fabulous opportunity to foster parent-to-parent networks. Building a strong classroom community will enhance the family-like feeling in your classroom and strengthen the sense that family members are an essential part of the learning community. As Ilene describes, "Recently, when we had a Publishing Party in our classroom, one student shared that his favorite part of the event was reading his story to the parents of the other children in the classroom."

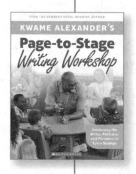

Jessica Lander

NOTE FROM JESSICA

Reaching Out to Your Families Before the Event

Jessica shares some advice about making personal connections with your families beforehand.

Remember to intentionally reach out and extend the invitation: "For Open House events, my enormous 3,500-student high school sends out robocalls. I've never found these particularly effective, though I understand why schools employ them. Building on the importance of invitations, I make sure to reach out to parents personally through phone calls or texts. I also make up colorful invitations, which I send home with my students. The first time I sent these invitations home, I feared that most would remain as a sedimentary layer in the bottom of my students' backpacks. Yet at my first parent Open House night, my classroom was filled with parents, many of them carrying the invitations I had sent home. In the end, it was only a small gesture—the real work comes in the conversations—but I believe it is important always to remember to actively reach out and invite parents personally.

Below we have included some icebreakers and activities that we believe might be helpful in planning for successful Back-to-School/Open House events that will begin creating community in your classroom.

Icebreaker: Who Am I?

This is a quick and often fun way for family members to swiftly make a connection with one other person in the room. It is also possible for family members to share one thing they learned about the person sitting next to them.

Take something out of your purse, shoulder bag, or pocket that you think represents you. Turn to the person sitting next to you and tell them what the article represents.

Icebreaker: Human Scavenger Hunt

This is a great way for families to get to know something about a number of others in a relatively short amount of time. You might have done such scavenger hunts with students in the first week of school; we believe they work great for Back-to-School/Open House events as well, because they encourage parents not only to speak with you, but also to learn more from their classroom community—the parents of their child's peers.

Create and print out copies of a scavenger hunt with six to eight statements such as the following: "Find someone who speaks two or more languages." "Find someone who loves to go to the movies." "Find someone who lives in the same neighborhood as you do." Give family members 10 minutes to find other family members and school staff who fit these descriptions.

In addition to fostering parent-to-parent relationships, these events are a great way to deepen your relationship with your students' families. But what should you say, especially when you will likely have a room filled with parents and too little time for long in-depth one-on-one interactions?

In your conversations with families in your classroom, it is most productive to limit your message to three key items. For example:

- Give families an overview of what children will be learning that year and the benchmarks for that grade level.

- From the overview, focus on one or two key learning goals for that year and discuss how you can work together to meet that goal. Ask families to share with you and with each other strategies that they may already be using at home to support this goal. Share a fun strategy with families, and if there is time, have them practice that strategy during the meeting (remember, adults learn new skills by practicing!).

- Let families know that you are serious about and interested in frequent two-way communication between you and them. Provide information about when and how you can be reached and when you will be asking families for help to support their child's learning. Let them know about upcoming events, including family conference times, publishing parties, or other opportunities.

Why only three key points? Ideally you want the conversation to be as interactive as possible, with ample time to hear from families. Emphasize to families that you do not want this or future interactions with them to be one-sided. Demonstrating this early on will encourage families to engage more fully with you throughout the year.

When choosing what to share with parents, think about strategies to bring them into the learning process and give them opportunities to engage with what is taking place in the classroom.

Ilene Carver

NOTE FROM ILENE

A Strategy for the First Family Event: "Hopes and Dreams" Letters

I have used this activity at many Back-to-School Nights, and it also provides a great start to Family Conferences (see Chapter 4). Our children need to know that our goals and expectations for them this year are deeply rooted in the hopes, dreams, and expectations of their families; that home and school are not two separate worlds. I like to ask parents to write a letter to their child, and then I display the letters on the classroom walls as visual reminders of the importance of families as part of our classroom learning community.

What you will need:
- Special letter-writing paper
- Phone or other device to take photographs

Ask families to write a letter to their child, expressing their hopes and dreams for their child during this school year.

Encourage the family member to write the letter in the language with which he or she is most comfortable. It is also important to say that you as the teacher are glad to write for any family who would prefer to share their hopes and dreams orally. When they are finished writing, take a picture of the child with his or her family member(s).

Hang the letters and photographs in the classroom for the rest of the school year as a reminder to the children that their families are a critical part of the learning community.

In my own classroom, I have found that throughout the year students will read and examine the letters and photos, not only from their own family, but also those of their classmates. I suspect your students will do the same.

NOTE FROM JESSICA

Adapting the "Hopes and Dreams" Letter for High School

Jessica Lander

I recently adapted Ilene's "Hopes and Dreams" letter for my high school classroom. Instead of having the letter hanging up around the walls, which might embarrass some teenagers, I asked families to write their child a letter and then seal and address it to their child. I kept the sealed letters in my desk until later in December and then handed them out to each of the students to read. From what my students and their parents told me later in private, they found the process very meaningful.

Jamila Nichols

A PARENT'S STORY

The Power of Hopes and Dreams

Jamila Nichols comments about the significance of the "Hopes and Dreams" letters.

I tell my children all the time what I want for them in school. With the "Hopes and Dreams" letters up in the classroom, it reminds Nyheema what Mommy wants her to do and Daddy wants her to do. They don't just hear it from us at home but they can read our words at school all year long.

Strategies for Partnering With Families Who Are Learning English

Language can be a barrier to the participation of all families. When you made your initial phone calls to families, hopefully you found out if you have family members whose primary language is not English. Once you know what you need for translation, you can try to make a plan to meet the needs of these families.

The options include: enlisting other families who speak the same language to provide translation, asking for the support of another staff member at your school, reaching out to community organizations that might have staff who speak your families' languages, and finding technology to assist with the task.

Myriam Ortiz, community activist and former Executive Director of the Boston Parent Organizing Network, recommends simultaneous-interpretation equipment to be very effective for family night group presentations and activities. Simultaneous translation allows you to have one or more bilingual translators who translate into a microphone; the speech is then transmitted to headsets that are provided for families.

It could be the case that, depending on your school's population and your principal's or your language capacity, you might choose to give the presentation in a language other than English, and have English speakers wear the headphones.

Final Thoughts

First impressions are so important in all strong and true relationships, and we want to make sure that you begin building your relationships with your students' families on the right foot—we can't stress this enough.

We hope that these suggestions will help you rethink or provide you with new ideas about how to reach out to families at the beginning of the year. We also encourage you to talk with colleagues both at your school and at other schools to hear what they are doing to connect effectively with families at the beginning of the year.

We realize that this will require a significant investment of time in the beginning of the year, and indeed in the months leading up to school. But we want you to see family engagement as part of your professional practice, as an integral component just as important as your lesson plans and your curriculum scope and sequence. We are confident that you will reap the benefits throughout the year.

PARTNERSHIP CLIP

Chapter 3: Your Colleagues Reflect

Listen to your colleagues reflect on their experiences with family engagment.

scholastic.com/PartnerResources

Reflection

What do you do to initiate strong relationships with the families of the children you teach?

Transform Your Family Conferences and IEP Meetings

Y ou have settled into a rhythm with your students and your curriculum. As you get deeper into the school year, you've likely had a Back-to-School/Open House event, and are hopefully strengthening your relationships with families through follow-up phone calls, emails, text messages, and possibly home visits.

Over the coming school months, you will have the opportunity to deepen your conversations and partnerships with families through both formal and informal events. In this chapter, we focus on two essential and more formal educator/family meetings—Family Conferences and Individualized Education Plan (IEP) meetings. Family voices and opinions have not always been valued in these meetings, and we want to stress here that they must be in order for these meetings to be successful. We hope to provide you with suggestions and ideas to help you transform these meetings into meaningful opportunities to partner with families.

Family Conferences

Family conferences may make you nervous; indeed, they tend to make everyone involved nervous. The conference between families and teachers is one of those traditional school hallmarks, a natural opportunity for teachers and parents to build partnerships; yet too often, parents, teachers, or both can come away feeling dissatisfied or worse, upset. In *The Essential Conversation* (2003), Professor Sara Lawrence-Lightfoot explains that parents often approach conferences with dread, worried about what a teacher might say about their son or daughter. On the flip side, teachers often worry that they are unprepared and feel that their competency as a professional is on the line. Without sufficient time to build the necessary foundational relationship with families, such meetings can boil down to being a one-way oral progress report with little real dialogue or discussion, instead of a two-way dialogue where both parties get to share and learn from each other.

PROFESSIONAL READING NOTE

Both of these resources offer step-by-step guidance as well as tools for conducting student-led conferences:

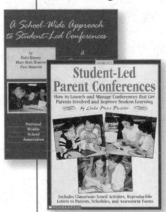

- *A School-Wide Approach to Student-Led Conferences: A Practitioner's Guide* by Patti Kinney, Mary Beth Munroe, and Pam Sessions; National Middle School Association, 2000.
- *Student-Led Parent Conferences* by Linda Pierce-Picciotto, Scholastic, Inc., 1997.

You also may want to download the following helpful documents from the Harvard Family Research Project:

- **Parent-Teacher Conference Tip Sheets, www.hfrp.org/var/hfrp/storage/fckeditor /File/FI-ConferenceTipSheet-111810.pdf.**
- **"Reimagining the Parent-Teacher Conference" by Heather B. Weiss, http://hfrp.org/publications-resources/browse-our-publications/reimagining-the-parent-teacher-conference.**

A national conversation about who should be involved in these conferences and how they should be run is taking place. We're seeing a movement away from parent conferences to parent-student-teacher conferences or student-led conferences. Such conferences can take many forms, but often involve students reflecting on their work, progress, and struggles in the weeks leading up to the conference, and then presenting this material and analysis to both their family members and their teacher.

There is a lot to be said for such a model—students are actively invited into important conversations about their education and urged to take ownership and to think intentionally about their learning and progress. Students have a structured opportunity to speak with their family members about their schoolwork, which may well spark more informal but similar conversations at home. What's more, involving students in the conference often leads to higher family attendance and participation.

Although student-led conversations are a big improvement over the traditional parent-teacher conferences, we would like to provide a model that we feel really builds on the funds of knowledge of all stakeholders, including family, school staff, and the student. Family conferences provide meaningful opportunities for teachers and families to speak as equal adults and partners in the work of supporting the student.

Why Family Conferences?

First, why are we calling them family conferences instead of parent conferences? As we stated in the introduction, we believe that the term *family* is more inclusive: It includes the student, but also may include any of the people who are important in the child's life, for example, a grandparent, an aunt or uncle, a godparent, or a cousin at the conference. By calling them *family conferences,* we signal to families that we want to include whichever members of the child's whole support network that the family wants present. We see the purpose of these conferences as creating space for collaboration. Each participant shares his or her perspective on how the school year is going and pledges to work together to support the child's continued progress. Finally, family conferences also can provide opportunities for students to reflect on their learning. In this way, the student presentation helps build strong relationships between school and home and creates an *extended learning family.*

Conferences are a critical component to building strong partnerships with parents centered on their child's learning. When well planned and thoughtfully approached, these conferences are an ideal opportunity to strengthen and deepen your partnerships with parents. But how to plan for a successful conversation?

Ilene Carver

NOTE FROM ILENE
A Tale of Two Conferences

Ilene describes her own experience as a parent attending starkly different parent-teacher conferences at two of her daughter's schools.

My daughter, Rachel, was a student in the Boston Public Schools from kindergarten through the 12th grade. When I went to Rachel's first Family Conference Night in her seventh-grade year, I was instructed to line up outside the classroom doors of her teachers. Rachel enjoyed Social Studies and I vividly remember standing behind a long line of parents as I waited to speak to her Social Studies teacher. After waiting for at least 30 minutes to speak with him, he shook my hand, said he was glad I was able to come, and that he thought he knew who my daughter was. I can still remember my incredulous state as I realized I had just spent a half hour waiting for absolutely nothing. While I did set up a meeting with the principal on a couple of occasions, I never attended a "family conference" again at Rachel's middle school.

When Rachel entered high school at Boston Arts Academy, it was an entirely different experience. Ms. Thomas, her advisor, had reached out to me weeks before and we scheduled a conference time that was mutually agreeable for the three of us, including Rachel. Ms. Thomas had gathered feedback from each of Rachel's teachers and we talked together about her progress across academics and her art, dance. We also had the opportunity to sign up for individual conferences with Rachel's other teachers. This meant we could meet with any teacher in the school for 20–30 minutes without standing in line, and that time would be ours. During Rachel's four high school years, I attended every family conference and relished the opportunity to collaboratively discuss my daughter's strengths and her areas for growth. She flourished at this school, and, as her parent, I felt respected.

We hope to give you the tools and have you consider the mindset necessary to make conferences successful for all involved, to be a key building block on your road to building partnerships.

The Difference Family Conferences Can Make

Naomi Bones

Naomi Bones, parent of a kindergarten and a second-grade student, describes the importance and value of inviting students to be part of the conversation.

The way we do family conferences at Dudley Street Neighborhood School makes it much easier for me to understand what needs to be done in order to get my child Jowell to reach the goals we set. My child is part of the meeting; he is not just sitting there listening to others talk about him. The students have to express their opinions about what their parent and teacher can do to help them improve. They can talk about any concerns they might have. We all work as a team to achieve the goals we establish together. I've never had a family conference like this; it makes a big, big difference.

Last year when we had a family conference at the school where Jowell was previously, Jowell felt like he was getting in trouble at the meeting. The teacher was mainly pointing out negative aspects about my son. Jowell felt unwanted because of the way in which things were being said to him, around him, and about him, and it turned him off from school. How his teacher thinks about him makes a major difference in Jowell's attitude and academic progress. He has done a complete 180 at Dudley Street Neighborhood School. I regret not having him here sooner. Jowell feels loved, he feels part of the community, and he's doing so well. Jowell knows we are a team, and he is a part of it!

The Value of Involving the Child

Camelia Toussaint

Camelia Toussaint, a parent of a second grader and a kindergarten student, talks about how having students at conferences is just as important as it is for parents to share with them their expectations and their hopes and dreams.

At first I wasn't used to having the child at our family conference because that is not usually how it's done. I was a little hesitant. But I also felt that having a conference without the child is kind of secretive. With the child being involved, it helps to feel like everyone is on the same page. Nathaniel knows what everyone is saying about him. He doesn't have to wonder, and if he hears something that he thinks isn't true, he can express that. I feel like hearing from his parents is important. It's not just the teachers who have the expectations; we do, too. It's a partnership, all three of us. I felt very proud to help Nathaniel set his goals and to hear the positive things he's doing in class. And because we stay connected, it helps with his behavior. If anything does happen, I'm in the loop. Last, Nathaniel knew he would be held accountable. When the parents are involved and working closely with the teacher, it's much better for all of us!

A PARENT'S STORY

The Power of Family Conferences

Rosa Larez

Rosa Larez, a fourth grader's mother, explains how important and powerful family conferences can be when done right.

When we had family conferences, you, the teacher, always asked me about my feelings, my thoughts, and what I understood about my son's progress; that made me feel like I was respected. You gave me the tools to help Vismark become a better student. It was special when you sent home books especially for him. I was able to sit with him while he read and I knew better how to help him. You know my first language is Spanish. For me, I think listening made the most difference. When I listened [to Vismark reading], it made Vismark want to read more. He was excited about the books he would bring home and he wanted to share them with me, too. Vismark felt proud of his progress and I felt proud of him, too.

As Ilene explains, "I work hard to make the point that our family conference is not just about the teacher telling the parent and student how the child is doing in school; rather, I want to hear how the child is feeling about her or his school experience and how the family is feeling as well. The conference is a time for each of us to report on progress we see and to ask questions and share concerns."

Why are these conferences so important? They give you an opportunity to expand on and maximize your family partnerships and share information and data with families. The family conferences also provide a space for families to share with you their experience and possible concerns. If the child needs support, you can work with the family early on to develop an action plan.

There are a number of ways to structure these conferences and conversations, and below we provide a possible outline. But if there is one essential to take away, it's the importance of creating space to listen to families and to build opportunities to work together throughout the year.

The Structure of a Family Conference

Here we provide a possible structure for your family conference. We have also included a Goal-Setting Family Conference Form that Ilene has developed over the years and uses in her conferences.

In preparing for these meetings, we suggest you gather examples of your students' work so you have them on hand to review with families.

Beginning

Start by making the conference interactive; begin by asking your students and their family members to share how the school year is going or what they like and dislike about their educational experience. Remember, you shouldn't be doing all of the talking, or even most of the talking. By having students and families speak first, you make it absolutely clear that your role as the teacher is to listen intently as well as to contribute.

Middle

Once families have had a chance to share, follow with your updates about how class is going, and share and discuss assessments and samples of student work. We hope you spend time looking *together* at this work. Don't forget to provide opportunities for your students to explain their work to their families and for their families to ask questions.

Ending

Toward the end of the family conference, we suggest asking the child to set a few goals for the next period (here we suggest using the Goal-Setting Family Conference Form). Together with their family, encourage students to choose a goal and talk about how everyone in the room can help the child reach that goal: what specifically the teacher can do, the family can do, and the student can do. Once this goal-setting process is complete, encourage everyone to sign the form.

Goal-Setting Family Conference Form

Name _____   Date _____

Teacher Comments (strengths/growth areas/concerns):

_____

_____

Family Comments (strengths/growth areas/concerns):

_____

_____

Student Comments:

_____

_____

Goal	What will the teacher do to meet this goal?	What will the scholar do to meet this goal?	What will the family do to meet this goal?

_____   _____   _____
Student Signature   Teacher Signature   Family Signature(s)

We believe these three-way goal forms are a powerful demonstration and reminder to students that parents and teachers are working together to support their success, and that there is shared responsibility. They are also a great way to help provide concrete opportunities for teachers and family members to work together.

A TEACHER'S STORY

A System of Support

Dara Bayer

Dara Bayer, a sixth-year teacher at Boston Arts Academy, speaks to the importance of showing students they have support from both teachers and parents.

I feel like [family conferences are a] space for us to integrate the worlds. At times, school may feel separate from the rest of a student's life. You can build a broader and more complex understanding of who the young person is, with both family members and teachers at the table. It makes it possible to create a broader system of support with everyone on the same page. Students reflect on "How am I doing?" and "How can I enable my support system to help me be successful?"

As Ilene describes, "We treat these goals like a contract. I make a copy of the Goal-Setting Family Conference Form for the family when the conference is complete so they can take it home. Many families tell me that they hang the form on the refrigerator so they can, at home, continue the conversation about the child's personal and academic goals. When I am writing the next report card or at a future conference, I make sure to report on the child's progress toward meeting his or her goals."

A TEACHER'S STORY

Combining Portfolio Presentations With Family Conferences

Nachelle Gordon

Some teachers have worked creatively to ensure enough time for family conferences. Nachelle Gordon, an English teacher and teacher leader at New Mission High School in Hyde Park, Massachusetts, describes linking family conferences to another classroom event.

We have two portfolio events a year and families come in to see their child's presentation. The students wear their best, most "professional" clothes.

Because their families are attending, the kids work hard to be prepared and to impress their parents. This is a chance for families to see what their children are learning, to understand their strengths and their struggles. In the portfolio process, families are not just observers; they can ask questions of their child at any time during the conference.

At the end of the student portfolio presentation, the conference begins and everyone weighs in. In this way, teachers get to see how much parents care and that fuels teachers' commitment to staying in close contact with the parents.

Reality Check

Clearly, family conferences are an essential component of strong, collaborative home/school partnerships. We want to emphasize that we have been outlining what we consider best practices, while realizing that your school may not give you sufficient time to hold these meetings, particularly for those of you who teach in secondary schools. You might be saying that at your school there is little or no time set aside for family conferences. If that is the case, we have a few suggestions:

- First, we urge you to speak with your administration and press for dedicated time to do this important work—and, in particular, strongly advocate for face-to-face meetings with your students' families.

- Another possibility could be to suggest that some of a school's mandatory professional development hours, particularly early-release days, could be repurposed as designated time for conferences.

If neither of these is possible, we have a few more recommendations and ideas:

- You can also choose to schedule family conferences on your own time—although we realize that you are likely already over-committed in the work you do for your students. Still, while conferences might seem like a lot of time up front, they pay huge dividends for you in your success with your students.

- While not ideal, you can also hold family meetings over the phone or via Skype. We urge you to organize and run these family phone conferences as though you were meeting in person. Try to hold a conference call (now easy on most smartphones) so that you can include family members and students. Early on, establish three-way sharing by having everyone taking a turn to share and speak; remember, this should not just be about you reporting out—seek out family perspectives and stories. As a teacher, try to include some specific stories and details from your classroom that you can share with each student's family. And finally, together try to establish a few shared goals. Another strategy that might help in these phone conferences is to send home a sheet the day before (similar to the kind you would use in an in-person conference) so that you and family members have something to reference during the call.

Even if your school does not provide enough time, we encourage you to try to set up a meeting with every family you can—perhaps before or after school, for the length of time to which you think you can commit.

We have stressed the importance of starting your relationships with your students' families early and on the right foot, and this is where those relationships will pay off. Families are more willing to participate in events later in the semester, like family conferences, if you've taken the time to build these partnerships early in the school year. If you find that attendance at these events is low, ask yourself if you have started to build relationships of trust and respect with your families.

IEP Meetings

Students with disabilities secured their right to education in 1975 with the passing of the Individuals with Disabilities Education Act (IDEA), landmark legislation that said that *all* children were entitled to "free and appropriate public education in the least restrictive environment required to meet their needs." Prior to IDEA, too many children with disabilities, both mental and physical, were simply locked away in institutions, hidden from view, and denied an education and a chance to create a meaningful life.

PARTNERSHIP CLIP

The Impact of Family Engagement on Student Success

scholastic.com/PartnerResources

It's likely that you, as a teacher, have received little or no training on how to engage with families in the IEP (Individualized Education Program) process. This is unfortunately all too common. The simple yet powerful strategies that you will read about in this section center around two essential ideas:

- **Mindset:** Believing that families must be partners in supporting students with disabilities

- **Communication:** Thinking intentionally about how best to ensure students' and families' legal rights; how to ensure fluid and regular two-way communication; and how to consistently create opportunities for increased collaboration

---

KNOW YOUR POLICY

Who Should Attend IEP Meetings?

Who must actually attend an IEP meeting? The law is indeed very specific about who must be in attendance:

- **The parent or family member**
- *At least one* **of the student's regular education teachers**
- *At least one* **of the student's special education teachers or special education providers**
- **A school district representative**
- **An expert who can interpret the evaluation results (this can be one of the people already mentioned)**
- **If the parent or school staff member would like, another individual/advocate who knows the student or has special expertise may attend.**
- **If necessary, the school must provide a translator to translate documents.**
- **If appropriate, the child can attend the meeting (starting at the age of 14, the child must be invited to attend).**

We all know from our professional lives that preparing for important meetings is essential. Before such a meeting, you most likely spent some time familiarizing yourself with some of the research; you probably created a list of goals you hoped to accomplish by the meeting's end and ideas for next steps. If you didn't prepare, you would likely feel lost or hesitant when you stepped into the actual meeting.

IEP meetings are tremendously significant in the lives of families and students, helping to shape students' educational futures and chances for success. Given their vital importance, it is crucial that we ensure that families have all of the tools and information they need to come to these meetings prepared and confident.

A TEACHER'S STORY
Using the IEP Process to Collaborate

Elizabeth Goncalves Wachman, a special educator for the past 24 years, urges teachers to see a myriad of ways they can invite families to become collaborators and coeducators in support of children with special needs.

Elizabeth
Goncalves
Wachman

Special education law and the IEP process are designed to protect children and families, yet so often the evaluation process is intimidating for families. Classroom teachers and special educators can make a huge difference with their actions. Teachers can and must reject the traditional power hierarchy in the IEP process, and commit to partnering with families to make the process inclusive and reflective of the expertise that both families and professional staff possess.

Family consent is needed to begin the evaluation of a child. Once a family makes a written request and identifies the area of concern, the school has 30 days to conduct an evaluation and another two weeks in which to hold a meeting.

Families are supposed to receive the reports on their child two days before the IEP meeting. This is really important because it enables the families to begin to learn about the results of the testing and evaluation. It also makes a big difference if a teacher or member of the special education team reaches out to the family in advance and talks to them about what questions and concerns they have.

At the meeting itself, teachers can help families understand the language of special education and work hard to keep out the jargon. While quantitative data and testing results lead to the understanding of some aspects of the child, it is also important to include a lot of stories and examples of student work so that everyone can access and contribute to the picture that is being created.

There is a formal part of the meeting where family members are asked to address how they see their child now and in the future. This can be asked in a rote way—or the input of family members can really shape the conversation and outcomes of the meeting. IEP meetings, for teachers and other professional staff, should be as much about listening as talking and sharing information.

Family and professional staff should collaboratively determine the goals for the child together, and the family should discuss what aspects of the goals they can help support at home. Family members can and should work together with school staff to create a list of accommodations that are needed for the child. Using a general list often does not speak to the specific needs of an individual child.

Teachers can also make sure families know their rights. When the finished IEP is sent home, the teacher/special educator should ask for feedback: "Please let me know what works for you and what doesn't." Families can accept or reject the whole IEP or part of it. If a family is not satisfied with the recommendations of the team, they can request an extended evaluation. Families need to know what their options are, and teachers can partner with families to ensure that they are aware of the range of possibilities.

Once an IEP is signed and the child is receiving support services, the special education staff is responsible for sending home progress reports to address the progress that the child is making regarding his or her goals. It is crucial that these reports are written in a way that families can understand and make clear which goals the child has accomplished and which he or she is still working on. There is no question that many students with special needs come back after the summer break with stronger skills than when they left. This is a result of family support and intervention that can grow out of this kind of collaboration between home and school.

Disabilities, Race, and Income

Not everyone is identified equally. In recent years, researchers have identified and noted an astounding overidentification of low-income students for special education in comparison to upper- and middle-class students and, specifically, an overidentification of black and brown students. Before we get into the best practices of setting up and running an actual IEP meeting, we believe it is important to acknowledge the very present inequalities found in disability identification.

In urban school districts across the country, it is common to find African American and Latino students, especially boys, disproportionately represented in classrooms for children with behavioral and academic challenges. Any discussion about how best to partner with families concerning the IEP process must start by acknowledging this injustice. One reason for examining our own biases, as we discussed earlier, is to make sure we don't inadvertently contribute to the misidentification of students. We believe that one of the enormous benefits of building partnerships with families is that it gives us, as teachers, the opportunity to expand our own knowledge of the breadth of histories, experiences, and cultures within our classroom communities. There is no question this positively impacts our ability to see our students from a strength-based perspective.

As a teacher, you may be the one who flags a possible learning or behavioral disability for further exploration by an IEP team. We believe it is very important that you understand the current dynamics and challenges. To do so, we suggest you review some of the following research:

- *Disproportionality: Inappropriate Identification of Culturally and Linguistically Diverse Children* (2008) from the National Education Association (NEA)

- *Looking Forward: Toward a New Role in Promoting Educational Equity for Students with Disabilities from Low-Income Backgrounds* (2009) by Thomas Hehir

- *Review of Special Education in the Commonwealth of Massachusetts* (2012) by Thomas Hehir and Associates

- *Truth in Labeling: Disproportionality in Special Education* (2007) from the National Education Association (NEA)

Chandra
Joseph-Lacet

A TEACHER'S STORY

Children of Color and the Challenge of Overidentification for Special Ed

Chandra Joseph-Lacet has worked in the Boston Public Schools for the past 18 years as a classroom teacher, special educator, teacher mentor, and coach, and as an administrator, she gives voice to why it is so important to understand the history of race as it is tied to overidentification of disabilities.

I never thought I'd end up in special education. How I became a special educator had everything to do with race and class. When I was a classroom teacher and resource room teacher, I can't tell you how many times I was sitting at meetings where everyone around the table was white, and the family members and I were the only people of color. The family might or might not have spoken, but I could see their bewilderment. After the meeting, I would approach the family, or the family often would ask me, "Can we call you?" In our school district and at our school, the racial composition of our special education staff, in particular, is not reflective of our families and students.

Interacting with the special education process can become a really scary place for people who may already have a negative, if not turbulent, relationship based on their experiences over the years. It's really hard to watch. It's really personal to the parent, and our meetings should be about that. I feel like I bring that to the work. I'm an advocate for children, I'm an advocate for families. I'm not the gatekeeper for special education.

The reality is "yes, kids of color are overrepresented." I think we need to do a better job as teachers. As teachers, we all need to see ourselves as responsible for ALL the students in front of us. We can't give over the responsibility of certain kids just because it's too difficult. It's the teacher's responsibility to understand each child as a whole person, and it's our responsibility to check our own lenses first: our teaching lens, our learning lens, our class lens, our race lens, and our culture lens—and we may need help on these. Schools needs to be more collaborative—where teachers don't feel like they are being pitted against each other—so they can assist one another. That's a structural piece and a cultural piece. The expectation in schools should be that we are going to help one another, because every teacher brings strengths.

To ensure that students with disabilities are given the best education, the law requires schools, teachers, and families to work together to create an Individualized Education Program (IEP)— a legal document that details a child's learning needs, the specific types of supports the school and teachers will provide, and how the student's success and progress will be measured. In the law, families are highlighted as critical players. However, too often families are not given an equal seat at the table.

Likely as not, when you, as a teacher, first read the language of IEPs, you found some of the jargon and procedures confusing. Many families feel just the same. They are confronted with unfamiliar language and vocabulary; they are also coping with strong emotions of concern for their child.

Imagine you have just been told that your child has a learning disability— you likely have a whole range of questions: What exactly does this disability mean and how does it affect my child? How will the school support my child? What kinds of supports can I give my child at home? Where can I find more information or connect with other parents of children with disabilities? Will this hurt my child's chances of getting into college? Of getting a job?

So now imagine what it might be like for the families in your school who have just heard that the school wants to evaluate their child for a possible disability. Too many parents have shared how they have felt excluded from decisions or intimidated by school staff, so that they feel as though their voice and opinions about the education of their child are not honored.

As teachers and as school administrators, we need to create space, time, and opportunities to hear and honor these essential questions. How can we become allies of our students' families? We live in an age where children born with a whole host of disabilities are no longer limited, and can do amazing things. To this end, a true family partnership—perhaps here more than anywhere else—is essential to ensure that all children have a real shot at realizing their full potential.

Adrienne
Wetmore

A PARENT'S STORY

Two-Way Communication Is Indispensable

A number of parents we spoke with who have children with significant learning or behavioral disabilities emphasized that regular two-way communication was essential. Adrienne Wetmore, the mother of a seventh-grader who attends the Young Achievers Science and Mathematics K–8 Pilot School in Massachusetts, describes how important this dialogue is.

One of the reasons I liked Young Achievers is because there is an open door. The teachers would allow me to come in and be with the kids at any time. My child had difficulties making friendships and I felt like my presence might have helped him to make friends. He needed a bridge.

The teachers understand my son and fight for what he needs. I don't ever feel like I'm not listened to. The teachers have advocated for my son to do the same things that every other seventh-grader has the opportunity to do. That's the kind of thing I look for. I get texts from my child's teachers if my son is having a good day and texts from the therapists if my son is moving forward. Communication is everything. I don't like not knowing. I have trust that is based on my experience of working together with the school for the best interests of my son.

Aracelis
Santana

A PARENT'S STORY

Echoing the Importance of Communication

Aracelis Santana, another parent at Young Achievers Science and Mathematics K–8 Pilot School, echoes the importance of communication, particularly for families who are more comfortable speaking in a language other than English.

The most important thing to me is that teachers communicate with me about everything. Some years I have had teachers who spoke Spanish, and that made communication easy. In other years, we have relied on the family coordinator, who is Spanish-speaking. Every form of communication has to be in my language.

Before I came to Young Achievers, I had a lot of trouble. Things would happen with my son and no one would communicate with me. I didn't understand what was going on. When my son came to Young Achievers in first grade, he was diagnosed with autism. Since then, the school has monitored his progress and kept me informed through meetings, phone calls, and written communication. What makes me feel respected is that whenever my son is facing an issue, the school meets with me, we talk about it, and together we decide what's best for him.

Adrienne Wetmore and Aracelis Santana both highlight the importance of communication with schools and teachers on an ongoing, sometimes daily, basis. But what about the actual initial IEP meeting? How can you transform this incredibly important but stressful meeting into a meeting that recognizes and honors the voices of families and reassures them that you and they can work together to support their child? Let's break down the meeting into four steps:

1. Setting up the meeting
2. Planning the meeting
3. Holding the meeting
4. Following up

Setting Up the Meeting

How do you reach out to families to ask them to attend an IEP meeting? How do you explain what the meeting is about? How do you inform families about what will be discussed, and how they can prepare? How accommodating are you about their schedule in finding a time to meet?

Planning the Meeting

Where do you hold an IEP meeting? Who is a part of the meeting? We have spoken in previous chapters about how schools can be intimidating places for families. In rethinking successful IEP meetings, we must consider the possible power dynamic that might exist between families and school staff. Not only can it be intimidating to come into a school space where the teachers and other professional staff are considered the experts, but it can be hard to challenge ideas or ask questions if meetings are set up as a school team versus a family. Being aware of these dynamics is the first step toward creating a new kind of meeting where everyone feels comfortable. No detail is too small to consider—beginning with how the meeting is set up and the agenda is created so that families feel as though they are part of the team, not auxiliary to the team, or even worse, an adversary.

Dr. William
Henderson

FROM THE PRINCIPAL'S DESK
Why We Must Put Families First

Dr. William Henderson, former principal of the Patrick O'Hearn Elementary School in Boston (since renamed the Dr. William W. Henderson Inclusion Elementary School), is a leader and pioneer in inclusive education. His former school became a model of what inclusive education can and should look like. In reflecting on the IEP process, Henderson is clear in his commitment to putting families first.

It's important that IEP meetings do not occur in a vacuum. We started with Karen Mapp's paradigm of "welcoming, honoring, and connecting" with families. Because we worked so hard on involving families generally—visiting new families at home and welcoming families to the school for conferences, math nights, classroom exhibitions, and performances—all that groundwork shaped our IEP meetings in ways that were positive and constructive. The quality of family involvement and interactions at the school really matters.

Other strategies that made a difference included getting families the IEP in advance—after all, this is their legal right, and reading through the plan in advance of the meeting allows families to ask questions; reaching out to families with a personal phone call, not just sending home an IEP meeting notice in the child's backpack; and making an extra effort to find out in advance what meeting time will work for the family. We tried to schedule IEP meetings at the best possible time for the family, and at a time that would also accommodate the staff.

IEP One-Pagers

While teachers aren't in charge of planning and running an IEP meeting, there are many proactive steps you can take to help create an environment where families are welcome as equal partners. One such strategy is to create a simple IEP one-pager, designed by Emma Fialka-Feldman, an inclusive elementary school teacher in her fourth year of teaching. Emma uses this IEP one-pager to highlight in jargon-free language what her students are working on, what types of supports they need, and what accommodations she recommends. She has found that these IEP one-pagers give the school staff an opportunity to reflect on the ways the individual with disabilities is growing and what next steps the school will be taking. Such a one-pager does not take the place of required forms, but it is a great place and less intimidating way to start off the conversation at an IEP meeting. Emma has found that the one-pager reduces the jargon of Special Education and helps to make these meetings more useful for all involved. What follows is an example of a one-pager that Emma has created, and also an example of a filled-out form.

Emma Fialka-Feldman

IEP ONE-PAGER: A snapshot tool to help the IEP team give a strength-based approach to discussing reports and progress.

Student's Name: _____

4 Things the Student Can Do INDEPENDENTLY:

Examples include:
- Follow a dramatic play sequence to engage with peers.
- Solve varied story problems by accurately visualizing the actions in the problems.
- Use tools to write complete sentences.
- Use the schedule and routine to anticipate social and academic expectations.

3 Things the Student is BEGINNING to Do:

Examples include:
- Monitor his reading (persevere through longer words and self-correct).
- Write her name.
- Count objects showing 1:1 correspondence.

2 Things the Student Can Do WITH SUPPORT:

Examples include:
- Sustain attention to independent work.
- Participate in academic class discussions and group learning, sustaining her attention to the topic.

During the School Year (Fall, Winter, or Spring), We Will Be Focusing On (list 2–4 skills):

Examples include:
- Continuing to develop skills to think flexibly and problem-solve confidently.
- Using technology to support her growth as a writer.
- Focusing on the skills of fluency and phrasing as a reader.

Key Accommodations We Use in the Classroom (list 2–4 accommodations that are essential for the student):

Examples include:
- Multi-step tasks broken into visual and simplified steps, with adult or peer modeling.
- Minimal language for redirection and reminders.

Include photos (3–5) of the child. These photos can help paint a picture of who the child is at school and can align with the ideas in the document as well.

Student's Name: Sarah

4 Things Sarah Can Do INDEPENDENTLY:

- Read for sustained periods of time and use text evidence to talk about the book.
- Advocate for herself when she needs adult support solving a problem with a peer.
- Write with a strong author's voice.
- Apply knowledge of phonics to decode words and write words.

3 Things Sarah Is BEGINNING to Do:

- Solve varied story problems by accurately visualizing the actions in the problems.
- Attend for greater lengths of time in whole-class instruction and participate actively.
- Read social situations during the school day and decide on appropriate times to communicate concerns or share knowledge.

2 Things Sarah Can Do WITH SUPPORT:

- Sustain attention to independent work.
- Solve problems over time, instead of immediately.

During the Spring, We Will Focus on:

- Skills of fluency and phrasing as a reader.
- Building stamina to increase task completion.
- Continuing to develop skills to think flexibly and problem-solve confidently.

Key Accommodations We Use in the Classroom:

- Frequent check-ins and prompts to return to task.
- Clear and consistent expectations and language.
- Preferential seating.

Holding the Meeting

Like a Family Conference, IEP meetings should be anchored in listening to each other and sharing goals. Particularly for students with IEPs who might need more support both at home and school, strong partnerships are critical. The IEP meeting gives you and your school—particularly the IEP team—a great opportunity to deepen your collaboration with families.

It can be easy, though, to let the regulations and legal requirements of IEP meetings dictate the structure of the meeting, making for a stiff and formal process that serves neither the family nor the teachers.

Dr. William Henderson

FROM THE PRINCIPAL'S DESK

Three Glows Before a Grow

Dr. Henderson proposes an alternate approach to structuring IEP meetings.

I remember when it was my second or third month as principal at the school, in 1989. After an IEP meeting that I hadn't attended, a parent asked if she could speak with me. (We had many students with disabilities and I attended some, but not all, IEP meetings.) This parent said to me, "I am tired of going to IEP meetings where teachers focus on all the stuff my son can't do, all his deficits. I know what he can't do. I want to hear about what he can do and what strategies they are going to use to help him." This conversation got me really thinking, and it led to a paradigm shift at the school. It became our policy, whether we were holding a family conference or at an IEP meeting, to begin conversations about students by focusing on their strengths, rather than their deficits—"three glows before a grow."

Successful IEP Meetings

Drawing on the advice of Dr. Henderson and Ms. Wachman, we suggest focusing on two key elements that we hope can help you, the IEP team, and families, have more successful IEP meetings:

- **Focus on Collaborative Goal Setting.** Much of the IEP meeting will be centered on identifying your student's particular strengths and areas in which he or she needs support, and creating procedures for classroom support or establishing types of accommodations necessary to support the student. How can families be an integral part of this process and this plan? What supports and what long-term goals can be addressed both at home and at school, and what strategies can families share with us that work at home and might be successful in our classrooms? Important, too, is not to lose sight of the long-term goals for each student and what we hope they can achieve. Together, families, teachers, and other members of the IEP team should construct these goals, drawing on the hopes and dreams of families, along with the identified growth areas for the student. IEP plans should revolve around reaching those goals, involving strategies both for home and school, and regular check-ins.

- **Avoid Jargon.** The world of education is brimming with acronyms and terminology. Immersed in this world, it can be easy to forget that most people (families, but also anyone else in another profession) are not familiar with these terms. Families, likely already worried and unsure about their child's disability, might feel less welcome to share their ideas, concerns, or questions if they are constantly trying to understand the jargon we are throwing (perhaps unconsciously) around. A few ideas Chandra Joseph-Lacet suggests: "Ask as many questions of families as you can. I watch body language. I watch eyes. I'll stop the meeting and ask, 'Is everything okay?' Sometimes, I can see there is something I need to address. I also will take the lead in asking specialists to clarify their reports. I will say something like, 'For those of us who are not OTs, can someone please explain?' I do this to make it more comfortable for the family members who are present, and also because sometimes I don't understand the language myself!"

Following Up

While regulations require a yearly check-in, we—and many other teachers as well—suggest making much more regular follow-ups with families, immediately after an IEP meeting and in the months that follow.

These can be both official and unofficial connections. At Dr. Henderson's school, he arranged it so that in certain cases, the whole team (staff and family) would meet three months after an IEP meeting simply to check in on all fronts and see how the student was progressing, rather than wait for a whole year to pass. Emma often uses the IEP one-pager as a guide for much more frequent check-ins via phone and text. She also uses the form to help her write up her IEP quarterly notes and report cards.

We hope that as you build close collaborations and partnerships with the families of your students, you will be in frequent communication.

Working With Families on IEP Meetings

What should the teacher expect as follow-up from the IEP? Who takes the lead next? Specifically:

- Special education teachers and whoever is assigned by the district to chair meetings are responsible for the goals and benchmarks on an IEP (this is not the classroom teacher). They are the ones who write the final document. In order for it to take effect, the family must sign.

- One way a classroom teacher can help in this process (but is not mandated to do so) is to reach out to the family to get the plan signed, or to gather feedback from the families to relay back to the IEP team.

- After the meeting, classroom teachers have a number of possible roles.

  - If they are dual certified and have a student with an IEP in class, they can be held accountable for implementing all or some of the goals on the IEP.

  - If they are not dual certified, they work with the special education teacher to modify curriculum where needed.

  - Most generally, classroom teachers implement accommodations laid out in the IEP or 504 plan.

Translation: Language, Power, and Social Justice

Schools can often be intimidating and alienating places for families, and can be even more so for new immigrants and families who speak little or no English. Throughout this book, we have talked about power hierarchies throughout the walls of our schools, hierarchies that can make it difficult for true collaboration between teachers and families. Perhaps nowhere is this more present than when families struggle to communicate in the primary language of the school itself.

It is essential that schools ensure that families are able to communicate in the language in which they feel comfortable, as we discussed in the Introduction and in Chapter 3. In the best-case scenario, your school is institutionally committed to making sure that translators are present or accessible for any kind of communication such as phone calls, conferences, or even notices home. However, we realize that this is often not the case. Your school might not have the resources or have prioritized translators. If so, there are still ways you can, in your classroom and in your community, ensure that families are able to communicate fully with you and you with them. One particularly effective strategy Ilene has found is to reach out to local community organizations, particularly those supporting immigrants. Often such organizations can be powerful partners, quite willing to help bridge the language divide. Ilene has partnered with community members to translate at family conferences and to accompany her on home visits in order to ensure that effective and respectful communication could take place.

Final Thoughts

Reflecting on the many strategies Ilene engages in across the year, she says, "Family conferences are my absolutely favorite thing to do all year. It is the place where we sit as a team and we put our heads and hearts together and strategize about what the next most important steps are in helping a child to be able to achieve all he or she can. There is a real intimacy to it."

Whenever you have a face-to-face meeting with family members—such as a family conference or an IEP meeting—it is a tremendous opportunity to:

- Break down the barriers that come from a result of historical hierarchy between home and school.

- Build relationships of trust and respect.

- Show that you really care about their child.

- Show that you value and respect the family's knowledge and contributions.

We can think of no better way of conveying to families that you are committed to working together as a team for the educational success of their child.

Reflection

- How do you convey to families that they are the "experts" when it comes to knowing their children, and make sure you learn everything you can from families to help you best teach each child?

- When and how do you share achievement data with your families, and how do you ensure that families also share their perspective on their child's progress?

PARTNERSHIP CLIP

Chapter 4: Your Colleagues Reflect

Listen to your colleagues reflect on their experiences with family engagement.

scholastic.com/PartnerResources

Maintain Strong Family Ties Throughout the Year

Effective family engagement never happens overnight—it is the result of hard sustained work over the course of a year. Up until now, we have focused on how to begin building relationships with your students' families, but how do you sustain and grow these relationships throughout the school year? How do you infuse your approach and your classroom events with the guiding mindset that parents are vital partners in the education of their children?

As you think about maintaining strong family ties during the school year, we would like to present you with four examples of strategies from four of your peers—teachers working in elementary, middle, and high schools:

- We Are All History Makers: The Family Story Project

- Breaking Bread: A Case for Family Potlucks

- Global Connection: Building Partnerships With Immigrant Parents Through Text Messaging

- Middle School Passage Presentations

In their own words, each teacher describes an important strategy they use to engage parents. Often they have reimagined traditional strategies—

potlucks, literacy nights, phone calls home—so that they engage parents in more meaningful and collaborative ways. We present these as four "mini case studies."

Common among these strategies are five guiding principles that help to transform traditional approaches into approaches that are grounded in the belief that parents are equal partners rather than observers. These four strategies presented by teachers are aligned with the five process conditions of the framework we laid out and discussed in Chapter 2. They…

1. are directly linked to learning.

2. strive to build and develop the relationships between teachers and parents, and between parents.

3. are inherently collaborative, with equal participation and input from teachers, families, and students.

4. honor families' home languages, cultures, and experiences.

5. strive to be interactive, providing many and varied opportunities to practice and learn together.

We hope that these teachers' voices, ideas, and thinking will help inspire you to create or reshape strategies and events that you can use effectively in your classroom. Most important, rather than simply describing the event, we have asked these teachers to reflect on how they approach this work, making their thinking visible. By sharing their approach, we hope they can model how you might go about creating and planning your yearlong approach to family engagement.

As you read each teacher's story, we suggest that you make a mental list of ideas, strategies, or approaches that you might wish to replicate or riff off of in your own classroom. We have asked each teacher to share experiences in his or her own words, but after each, we encourage you to take some time to reflect on your own practice. To guide and support you in this reflection, we pose a series of questions for you to consider.

PARTNERSHIP CLIP
Maintaining Powerful Family Partnerships

scholastic.com/PartnerResources

We Are All History Makers: The Family Story Project

The history lessons taught in our schools are often incomplete stories, leaving out many rich details about the contributions and cultures of the children whom we serve in our classrooms. Traditionally, schools have focused on teaching the stories of those in power, but in doing so they send the message (often unconsciously) that the lives and histories of their students and their families are less important. Of course, this is completely untrue.

Early in her teaching career, Ilene found a way to tap into the lives and stories of her students. Wanting to make it clear to students that their stories and families were part of a rich history and an important part of their learning, Ilene sought a way to bring her students' families' expertise into the classroom. Below, she describes the Family Story Project and the curriculum she created.

One effective way I've found to engage families is by implementing curriculum that puts families at the center of what children are learning. Early in my teaching, I developed a unit that focused on family stories.

Ilene Carver

There has been a raging debate across our country about what history is essential for young people to learn. In my opinion, what is critical for our children to know is that the experiences and stories of their families, often excluded from traditional textbooks and curricula, are an important part of "history." All of us must understand that we are history makers in order to believe we can affect the course history takes. Including a curriculum like this sends a powerful message. It says to families, "Your history, culture, and experiences are valued in our classroom. They are a part of the knowledge that we believe all children should know."

Since then, I have used a family story curriculum with students from kindergarten through fourth grade. Generally in my family story units, the guiding questions have been: "Where do I come from?" and "How does my history and culture shape who I am?" But the guiding questions for such a unit can also vary depending on the focus.

Across the grade levels, the project begins with students interviewing their families. When I teach younger grades, these student interviews are supplemented by teacher interviews with each family as well. I have created a written questionnaire that students can use with their family members. But for the younger grades, I often help support my students—I usually find that the best way to gather information is by talking to the families by phone, or even better, face-to-face. I have often interviewed family members for this project at the first family conference in the fall.

When making a questionnaire for young students, I include such questions as:

- When did your family come to Boston?
- Where did your family come from? What was life like there?
- How did your family travel to Boston (by bus, train, car, boat, airplane)?
- What neighborhood does your family live in?
- What qualities or values are important to your family?

Students, especially in the older grades, will also add their own research questions that they are curious about to ask their families.

Once we have the information, the children work on "telling" their story. For the younger children, there is a major emphasis on constructing a three-dimensional model of their family's story. I'll have students divide pieces of cardboard (or cut paper) into sections so the children create representations of where their family came from, the vehicle they traveled in, their current neighborhood, and something that is important to their family now—their home, place of worship, school, the kinds of food they eat, and so on. Some years, the children have built these representations with plasticine, pieces of wood, milk cartons, or cloth and yarn.

The first year I did this project, I was working at the Mission Hill School in Roxbury, Massachusetts. That year, I co-taught with longtime Boston kindergarten teacher Alicia Carroll, and we created this curriculum together. One student, Gerrell, used cardboard to construct the R. J. Reynolds factory where his grandfather had worked in North Carolina. Abdirizak crafted the car with figures of the eight members of his family who had escaped the Civil War in Somalia by driving to a refugee camp in Kenya before traveling to the United States. Another student, Emily, made her model to tell the story of an ancestor who had been an indentured servant on the *Mayflower*, and Antonia made one of the cotton fields of South Carolina, where her grandmother had picked cotton as a young girl.

In the older grades, the children write what they learned from their family interviews in addition to constructing a three-dimensional model of their story. Often, we make a time line to help us understand how long ago each family came to Boston. This also becomes the basis for math story problems that are highly engaging for everyone in the classroom community— including students, school staff, and parents. While we work on these math problems primarily at school, some of the work goes home for students to engage in directly with their families.

The unit always ends with a classroom presentation with families and students. Family after family rises to share their stories, usually with the child and a family member each telling a different part. Few history books tell these stories, and none are written for very young children. These family gatherings enrich and deepen our understanding of the multiracial, multi-ethnic community in the classroom, for the children and adults alike.

Reflect and Act

- How do your current family engagement activities integrate the culture and stories of the children's families?

- Are there ways that you can create opportunities for your students to engage their families in their learning assignments?

- What two or three ideas will you take from this teacher's strategy to add to your own practice?

Breaking Bread: A Case for Monthly Potlucks

Family potlucks, particularly held in elementary school classrooms, are a staple school event. But, too often, they resemble a traditional parent open house, with families who don't know each other waiting to speak briefly with the teacher. Consequently, these events fall short of building community and strengthening relationships around student learning. In addition, such events unintentionally exclude parents and families with less flexible schedules.

Meg Bruton, a veteran 25-year kindergarten teacher, has transformed these traditional potlucks into monthly, more informal gatherings. By making these events regular and informal, Meg has found that the potlucks have helped to foster connections between parents and families in her class, as well as deepening her own relationships with her students' families. Below she describes her monthly potlucks in her own words.

Meg Bruton

When I first started teaching, I wondered how I'd be able to grow the relationship between home and school not only for my students and families, but also for me. We had biannual parent-teacher conferences and the occasional calls home, or meetings to discuss issues a child might be having at home or in school. When the Internet arrived, so, too, arrived the many vibrant classroom blogs detailing the inner workings of our room, quick emails dashed off about scheduling for students, heads-ups about rough nights at home, playground issues, and the concerns or joys a parent might be having with his or her child. The Internet clearly provided us with a quick connection to each other yet; how was I going to build community with parents around the classroom, in person? How could I make connections with those parents who felt too shy to email or were too busy? How could I help parents get to know each other? The school culture gave us another opportunity. Every so often, classrooms would have morning breakfast potlucks. Those parents who could do so would drop in for a bit, chat with other parents, poke around the classroom, have a bite to eat or some coffee or tea, and then head off to work. While these events seemed like a good start, I knew that if we were to really build connections, these needed to happen with more frequency for the children and the parents.

Once we scheduled out these potlucks for the year, working parents could schedule ahead of time the potlucks they could attend, and not feel guilt or shame if they could get only a few in during the year. Some gatherings would be informal, a "walkabout" in the room, and others might have a focus, "Celebration of Lights" or "Poetry Share" or "Art Share" or a play we might perform. Parents could do some of the activities we had set out or were exploring. Parents saw work on the walls, and drawings and writing journals tucked away in cubbies. We'd send out a sign-up list for families to share in bringing healthy foods and drinks—always making sure that the person who brought coffee came on the early side! We'd even have cleanup help, with the students doing their share. Having jobs gave everyone a chance to pitch in at some point in the year and feel a part of the event. We'd have name tags for families that could be reused again and again. And we hung family photos up on the walls all year long, helping other students and parents connect the dots on who belonged to whom.

For many, these potlucks felt like a natural extension of their preschool co-op experience, where being in the school and room happened with more frequency. For others, the potlucks would be a new habit of connecting with their child in school. They would set a warm and relaxed tone for the room, hopefully breaking down barriers as we got to know each other a bit. It would give me a chance to connect with those parents who were more shy, who took up "less space," who might be harder to reach via email, whose only connection with school was a negative one. It gave parents an informal parenting group to talk about their struggles and joys with each other. Children would get to see their grownups making connections with me and other parents.

There would be a mutual benefit for parents and for me, as their child's teacher. I would see interactions that helped inform my understanding of their relationships, and parents might see me modeling expectations and strategies with their child that were newer for them. I can't underestimate the power of parents seeing a teacher have enthusiasm for these gatherings. It broadcast in subtle and not-so-subtle ways that I not only enjoyed their children, but them, too. If a parent was in a rough spot with a child, having another adult show affection and real interest in the child while also acknowledging their own struggle helped parents see the child separate from a particular behavior that was weighing them and the family down. The "it takes a village" sentiment could really thrive at these potlucks. I made sure to inform all the office folks, those in the administration as well as specialists, to try to poke in and say "hi."

For children, the pride they had in showing their room and their learning was powerful, and built independence and ownership over their learning space. For parents, investment in the room and their relationship with me grew naturally. It took time, as any true relationship does, yet the levels of our conversations about their children were deeper and more trusting and honest. While parents looked to me for advice, I gained so much from them. I wanted them to know that they had a voice in the room, and a place. These gatherings kept conversations ongoing and not just relegated to the formal discussions held biannually. I know that they were crucial in building community, at any age.

Reflect and Act

- Do your family engagement events create opportunities for families to network with each other?

- How often do your students get to see you interacting with their families in the ways described in this teacher's strategy?

- What two or three ideas will you take from this project to add to your own practice?

Global Connection: Building Partnerships With Immigrant Parents Through Text Messaging

You are likely familiar with the teacher phone call, email, or now, text message sent home that fills parents or students with dread. Parents assume teachers are calling home because something is wrong, perhaps their child misbehaved. And for decades, and in many schools today, this remains primarily true. But these technologies are inherently two-way communication opportunities and have great potential for extending invitations to parents to engage with their child's classroom learning.

Jessica found that text messages—when rooted in the core beliefs we discussed in Chapter 1—can be an incredibly powerful and simple tool for reaching out to and fostering relationships with her students' parents. Family engagement is often weaker in high schools, and high schools, unfortunately, often focus less energy and time in inviting families into the school. Jessica has found that text messaging helps her learn from her students' parents and keeps them up-to-date on the goings-on of her classroom. Most important, as an EL teacher with students speaking over 30 languages, texting has allowed her to build partnerships with parents who have limited or no English. Below, she describes her approach in her own words.

High school students often tend to share less of their academic lives with their parents. Even if you are not a parent, you are likely familiar with the canonical conversation: "How was school?" "Fine." End of conversation. Research shows us that family engagement usually drops off in middle school and even more by ninth grade. Yet when asked, teenagers say they wish their families were more involved.

Jessica Lander

Engaging with a child's classes can be particularly challenging for parents who speak little or no English, and who might feel otherwise shy to reach out to teachers. As a high school EL social studies teacher, my students hail from over 40 countries, from Cambodia to Colombia. They speak over 30 languages. I speak only basic Thai and Kiswahili, and a little Khmer. I knew I needed to rethink how I could successfully communicate with my students' families, and how I could build a strategy for inviting them to partner with me.

In recent years, technology in school-focused text message apps has exploded. The development has been particularly transformative for engaging EL families—I can now translate a text message into over 80 languages. Suddenly I had a way to reach all my families in their languages and for them to reach out to me.

But technology (and communication) alone does not make instant successful family partnerships. How could I invite families to engage? How did I make it clear that I wanted to collaborate with and learn from them? How can I use this technology to provide more than progress updates?

I try to write text message invitations, creating opportunities for families to not only learn about their students' academic lives, but to partner with me in their child's classwork and to create a space from which I can learn from them.

Such texts might be simple: pictures from a presentation of Holocaust memorials that my upper-class students created, or questions parents might ask their son or daughter about what might "push" immigrants from a country, or "pull" them to another. I send these out once every week or two. I have been surprised and excited by the countless messages back that say simply "Thank you for including us," "Thank you for keeping me in the loop," "Thank you for letting us participate in this work that is so important to us."

Our conversations have created opportunities for parents to be distant teachers in my class. One morning, a student sidled over to me. "Ms. Lander," he said, part amused and part incredulous. "You texted my father!?" "What did he say?" I asked. "He asked me to name and explain the three branches of government, and then when I couldn't remember them all, he had me pull out my notes and made me review each with him."

Another night, I received perhaps the best text message I have ever gotten from a student. It read: "When your teacher tells your father about a PowerPoint presentation"; with it she had sent a photo of their presentation projected on their TV. As I learned the next morning, her father had made her practice again and again until she had it down perfectly.

Most important, our text conversations have allowed me to learn so much from my students' families, in a way that would have been much more difficult even a few years earlier given the language barrier. We share strategies on supporting a shy girl, or a boy who serially forgets his homework. I have been able to learn more about my students' histories and backgrounds, all of which have enabled me to support them better in class.

And, as the research suggests, our teenage students do want and need their families to be part of their academic life—even if they might not always say it outright. Late last spring, over a flurry of text messages, one mother planned with me to surprise her children, both students in my class, at a presentation they were giving at the State House. They had no inkling that she would come, but the look on their faces when they saw their mother appear was a resounding validation of how important this work is.

Reflect and Act

- How have you used text messages and other social media to reach out to families?
- How have you used this media (or how could you use it) to connect families to student learning?

- How can you think meaningfully and creatively about making sure that you are doing powerful outreach with families who speak languages other than English?

- How can you engage families who speak languages other than English to create partnerships that are as rich as the ones with families you can communicate with in English?

- What two or three ideas will you take from this project to add to your own practice?

Middle School "Passage" Presentations

Many of the strategies we have described work well even at the single classroom level. But when whole schools become invested, the door opens for an entire rethinking and repositioning of the role of families.

Lindsay Slabich was a founding history teacher at the Springfield Renaissance School in Springfield, Massachusetts, teaching grades 6 through 12. For the past five years, she has been an instructional leader at the same school. Lindsay has been deeply moved by the power and impact of true family partnerships when the entire school is invested. Her school has committed to family engagement by putting families front and center in the academic lives of their students. They make this clear in public ceremonies and milestones that the students go through, where families are not only asked to attend and cheer from the sidelines, but also are woven into the very heart of the ceremonies themselves.

On the following pages, Lindsay describes the culmination of the eighth graders' transition from middle to high school. Throughout the year, the students work with teachers and their families to construct a portfolio that includes: 1) a letter to a high school teacher in which they reflect on their growth in maturity and work over the stretch of middle school; 2) a personal reflection where students choose an object, quote, or song that demonstrates something about them; and 3) three reflective pieces on different pieces of academic work from their class, commenting on their craftsmanship, communication skills, and creative thinking.

From Lindsay Slabich:

Lindsay Slabich

It is May at the Springfield Renaissance School. Over the course of the month, families—cousins, nephews, little sisters just learning to walk, stepfathers, aunts—of all 100 of our eighth graders visit the school, many with balloons and flowers or trays of homemade rice and beans, cookies, and sandwiches. They come to witness and celebrate their eighth graders' passage presentations. Students have worked throughout the year, largely in crews (their daily advisory) to prepare. They must successfully pass this assessment in order to move on to ninth grade.

Thirteen-year-old Yessie, professionally dressed in a skirt and blouse, stands in front of the room and introduces her panelists to each other: "My grandma, who I call my mom because she has taken care of me since I was three, my brother, who is in college in Philadelphia, my real mom, who came from Boston to see my passage, my mentor and friends from my church youth group, my old principal from elementary school, my friends Julia and Angie, my English teacher, Ms. Cote, and my crew teacher, Ms. Slabich." The panel represents Yessie's family, the people at school who support her, cheer for her, and challenge her, and those from home, related and not, who do the same. Our job is to determine whether she makes a strong enough case that she is ready to move on to high school.

As Yessie continues to reflect, she tells us that, though she is still a "wild child," she is much better at staying in control when she feels angry or frustrated. She discusses her work habits and explains that she has grown the most in "actively and respectfully participating in class" but is still challenged by "assessing and revising her work." She passes around projects: one, a social studies essay in which she compared life for a colonial child growing up poor in New England to a poor child from the South; another, a math project that involved creating a geometric quilt. This work demonstrates mastery of the academic standards. As we view the work, Yessie shares thoughtful and thorough reflections about the process of completing the work and what it shows about her as a learner. As it is passed from family member to family member, her mother takes her time with it, reading each word, noticing the knowledge, the details, and the care put into it.

When Yessie's presentation is finished, we cheer; then we give her feedback. Her grandmother, tears streaming down her face, tells Yessie how proud she is. Her former principal, Dr. James, raises her hand. Yessie has invited this principal because when Yessie was in elementary school,

Dr. James made her feel that she would never be successful. Yessie invited her to prove her wrong and knows that she did just that. Dr. James praises Yessie for how far she has come. When the formal presentation is over, Yessie's grandmother approaches Dr. James and gives her a hug. She tells the woman she encountered so many times for negative reasons how proud she is of Yessie. This moment has made all of those trips to elementary school worth it. The room is filled with celebration, for Yessie's courage, her honesty, her reflectiveness, and her poise.

What a significant, empowering moment for Yessie and her family. Yessie's presentation has brought her family together into this space, where they have gotten to know Yessie in a different, more intimate way. Instead of the struggling wild child about whom teachers and counselors called home regularly, they saw a blossoming learner and a courageous young person. They began to understand that Yessie, at 13, was an agent in her own learning process, and that although she would still make mistakes, she was truly ready to take that control. It is clear as Yessie, her mom, and her grandmother walk out together that they are leaving with a new feeling of pride, a sense of hope for the future, and a shift in their understanding of themselves as a family.

Reflect and Act

- How are families meaningfully engaged in grade-to-grade or school-to-school transitions at your school?

- What are ways in which you can reshape academic projects so that families play a central and essential role and are not just there as fans standing on the sidelines?

- What two or three ideas will you take from this project to add to your own practice?

Final Thoughts: Other Ideas and Strategies

There are naturally a plethora of events and strategies that you can employ in your classrooms and in your work as a teacher. Below, we have amassed a list of other strategies we can use to engage with families throughout the year. By no means is this an exhaustive list. As these four teachers have done, it is not enough simply to hold these events; you must also thoughtfully consider how to create the events so that they meaningfully connect families to their children's learning and to the greater school community.

Elementary School

- **Publishing Parties:** A great way to honor students' work and to create meaningful opportunities for students to share their learning with families is to hold a publishing party. At the end of a unit of writing (personal narrative, poetry, research, etc.), you can work with students to "publish" their writing in "books." These books are then revealed at a culminating party where families are invited to come hear the stories and work their children and their children's peers have created.

- **Family Math Night:** One way to continue building the bridge between learning at home and learning at school is to hold a "Family Math Night" (or similar event on another school subject). Families are invited into the classroom, and the students have the opportunity to teach their family members math games that they have been learning and playing throughout the year. It also provides an authentic opportunity for students to take ownership and pride in their learning. At the end of the night, you can continue this learning by sending home a Family Math Night packet that includes the games and the necessary materials. In this way, families can continue to support their child's learning at home. Note: When whole schools can host a math night, it can give families opportunities to see what their child will be learning in future grades and years.

- **End-of-Year Celebration:** Academic celebrations are incredibly important and essential events that families must be an integral part of. They can take many forms, at both the classroom and school levels. At the classroom level, teachers might hold award ceremonies—gathering the learning community to recognize the child's academic achievements and making awards that recognize each child's unique contributions and strengths. This also can be a powerful opportunity to invite parents to help lead and create such events and particularly to participate and speak. Some schools hold school-wide celebrations where students as a classroom perform poems, songs, or other work that reflects their learning for the year. Such celebrations also can be used as a way to make the process of moving up a grade tangible and significant.

Middle School

- **Parent Panels:** Schools have long drawn on the strengths and assets of families to help teach lessons on a wide range of topics. But some schools have taken this a step further, inviting parents to come to class as the experts, either presenting solo to a class or on expert-family panels to share experiences from their work, and in the case of immigrant families, of their countries and journeys to the United States.

- **Plays:** Theater is a natural entry point to expand the community of teachers and educators to families, drawing on a wide range of expertise and assets. At some schools, the play process will become a community group project, with families running different components. Because of the typical structure of plays and play practice, there are often many more opportunities for families with busy schedules to participate. Some schools have had great success in having students write and perform their own plays that draw on their personal family stories, thus providing further opportunities to engage and honor families in students' academic lives.

- **Adolescent for a Day Experience:** An interesting strategy being used at a number of schools is to invite families in for the morning and have them experience what it is like to be a student in the classroom. This can be done with students helping to show families around. Particularly at the middle school level, where students might be more resistant to sharing their school lives with their families, this strategy welcomes parents to see and experience their child's school lives. Schools have successfully structured classes around peer-to-peer seminars, creating natural spaces where teachers and parents can learn from each other.

High School

- **Student Exhibitions:** Creating a community event to celebrate the culmination of a class project or a unit of student work can be a successful way to invite families into a student's academic life at any age. It can be particularly impactful in high school, when families are not often asked to be a part of the life of the school. Such exhibitions can take many forms: a publishing party, a display of science experiments, or even an art show of student work. They provide authentic motivation for students and opportunities to take pride in their work in front of friends and family. If possible, consider trying to bring the event into the community itself—hosting the event at a local store or venue, which might make it more possible for community members to come and also make the experience more special for students.

- **Identity Assignments:** A powerful way of teaching students to appreciate and draw on the wealth of resources in their communities and families is to fashion projects, assignments, or even smaller one- or two-night homework assignments that push them to learn directly from their communities. Projects could include researching family foods and recipes (learning about the history and recipes that are important to families, writing stories or accompanying oral histories, and even cooking and sharing the food with the class); or surveying families to get a wider perspective on political, global, and environmental issues. All such assignments aim to honor and draw on families' knowledge, and to reinforce for students that their families and communities are an integral part of their academic learning.

- **Creating Community Change:** There are a growing number of comprehensive and well-developed curricula and organizations focused on teaching students to create change in their own communities. Such organizations include Generation Citizen (generationcitizen.org), and Youth Participatory Action Research (yparhub.berkeley.edu). By taking lessons out of the classroom and into the community, students are encouraged to seek out the expertise of families and community leaders, learning to see them as valuable teachers and allies in their own pursuit of creating an impact in their city or town.

PARTNERSHIP CLIP

Chapter 5: Your Colleagues Reflect

Listen to your colleagues reflect on their experiences with family engagment.

scholastic.com/PartnerResources

Reflection: What opportunities do you provide for families to participate in their children's learning over the course of the school year?

CHAPTER 6

Support Your Work With Family-Friendly Resources

After reading this book, we hope you share with us the belief that strong family engagement is essential for the success of our students, the success of our schools, and the success of our individual practice as teachers.

Throughout this book, we have provided you with the voices of teachers and parents from across the country whose work and success have been transformed by meaningful partnerships. Whether you are new to this work or an old hand, we hope we have given you new ideas and tools to approach, begin, and continue this lifelong work.

To do this work well, you will need to reach out into your community and find and build alliances—connections with other teachers, school staff, school administrators, parents, students, and community organizations. With hard work, these connections and networks will help you expand your work and your impact on your students. It is incredibly important to have these various community partners to learn from and to lean on.

Powerful family engagement tends to have a ripple effect across a school and community, transforming mindsets and approaches. For those of you who are working in schools that do not yet partner with families, remember this: The work you do can have an enormous and positive long-term impact on helping to change the culture of your entire school.

Last, it is important to take time to nourish your body and mind. Again and again throughout these pages, you have heard from teachers who have shared how important family engagement has been for their practice and success. But we also realize that this work takes time and enormous energy. We are asking you to do hard and challenging work. We are asking you to be deeply self-reflective and, in many instances, to step outside your comfort zone. Point-blank, this work is and will continue to be challenging. Thus, it is incredibly important that you develop strategies to make sure you are taking time to rejuvenate yourself. Whether it is working in a weekly exercise schedule, taking time to read for pleasure, or setting up regular meet-ups with friends, making sure you are healthy and happy will have a direct impact on how much energy and focus you bring to this work.

Additional Tools to Build Powerful Partnerships With Families

To support you in this important and lifelong work, we have assembled some additional tools and resources to help you build powerful partnerships.

Tool #1: Sending "You Can" Letters to Families

This letter can be used to help introduce and engage families with the material their children will be learning in your class and provide them with concrete invitations to be part of this learning. Ilene and her colleagues create these letters to give out to families at Open House Night. Their hope is to provide to families an overview of what their child will be learning throughout the semester or year. It is by no means meant to be comprehensive, but rather to paint a general picture. A key element Ilene makes sure to include is a specific and clear "You Can" section with concrete ideas of how her families can help support their child's academic work at school.

What Our Grade 2 Scholars Are Working On in READING

- *Building Reading Stamina.* The goal is that by later in the year, kids will be able to read for 45 minutes (at home or at school). Right now, our second graders are reading independently for close to 20 minutes each day.

- *Comprehension, Accuracy, Fluency, and Vocabulary Building.*

  - We teach the importance of stopping to check for understanding (tell me what you just read).

  - We teach students cross-checking (Does it look right? Does it sound right? Does it make sense?).

  - We teach students to read fluently or smoothly so it sounds like talking. One way to practice is by repeated readings of one page of a book or of a poem.

  - We teach students to make note of interesting words and to try to use them in speaking and writing.

You can: talk with your children about what they are reading. If they get stuck on a word, you can ask them to try to figure it out by using "cross-checking." You can ask your child to read out loud to you so they practice fluency.

The research is clear: Children who read inside and outside of school daily make the most progress with reading and in all school subjects.

You can: help make sure your children read for at least 20–30 minutes each night and fill out their Home Reading Log.

What Our Grade 2 Scholars Are Working On in WRITING

Narrative writing (telling stories) about real things in their lives, as well as *opinion* and *informational writing.*

- We teach students to write in an organized way across five or more pages—stories that have a beginning, middle, and end, with lots of details and strong words.

- We teach students to spell high-frequency words correctly and use spelling patterns (such as *er, ly, tion*) to spell. We also teach students to use punctuation and capitalization, as well as quotation marks for dialogue, and the apostrophe with contractions such as *can't* or *don't*.

You can: ask your scholars to describe something they see/experience, or ask them about their opinions on something and why they feel that way.

What Our Grade 2 Scholars Are Working On in MATH

- Reading and writing three-digit numbers and comparing numbers using < and >.

- Being able to add and subtract two- and three-digit numbers, and explain how they solved the problem in writing and in class discussions.

    1. Being able to count to 1,000 using 5s, 10s, and 100s.
       Being able to tell time in five-minute intervals.

    2. Being able to count all kinds of coins up to several dollars.
       Knowing from memory all addition and subtraction facts within 20.

- Being able to accurately divide a shape into halves, thirds, or fourths, and use fraction notation.

- Using a ruler to measure to the nearest inch.

- Collecting data, creating graphs or other representations, and interpreting results.

You can: ask your scholars to help you count your change, skip-count by 5s, 10s, or 100s, tell time, and explain to you how they solved the addition and subtraction problems they received for homework.

Tool #2: Calling Home Guide

This sample script below can be used to help you make your beginning-of-the-year phone calls to families. Particularly if you are new to this work, a phone script can be a helpful guide to support you during these initial and very important phone calls (the kind we describe in Chapter 3). We urge you to make these calls as early in the year as you can.

Sample Phone Script

If English is not a language the family is comfortable speaking, find out what the preferred language is and call back when you have someone to help you translate the call.

Hello, my name is _____ and I am going to be your child's teacher at the _____ School this year.

We know that when families and teachers work closely together, our children achieve the most success. I am excited to be working with you this year.

Can you please tell me about your child, and be sure to let me know anything that you think I need to know that will make his (or her) year the best it can be?

Please tell me the best phone number to reach you and what time of day works best for you. Also, please know that I'll be calling from time to time to share with you your child's progress and to tell you about the important events at the school. Don't think when you see my number come up on your phone that it means there is a problem!

Do you like to communicate by text and/or by email? Here is the best way to reach me: _____. If you want to call me, please call between these hours: _____.

Is there anything else you want to share with me about your child?

Thanks for your time! I can't wait to see your child on (date of first day of school) and begin our work together.

Tool #3: Two Letters of Introduction

This tool is a way to help you reach out and connect with families on the first day of school. Ilene created this letter to introduce herself to families, share her contact information, and make clear her school's strong belief that children do their best when families and teachers are partners. While Ilene's example letter is directed toward the parents of students in second grade, Jessica has written similar letters to the families of her high school students, and includes one on the next page.

Dear Second-Grade Families,

We are delighted to be teaching your child in second grade this school year, and we are eager to get to know you as well. We believe that each child does his or her best when families and teachers work closely together.

In Gallaudet, the lead teacher is Emma Fialka-Feldman. She will be assisted by Boston Teacher Resident Maya Taft-Morales, and by Dudley Promise Corps member Tracy Curtin. In George Mason, the lead teacher is Ilene Carver. She will be assisted by Boston Teacher Resident, Nanna Waldroup and by Dudley Promise Corps member Xavier Villalona.

We have spoken with many families already, but in case we have not reached you, we want you to be sure to have our phone numbers. Ms. Carver can be reached at 555-555-5555 and Ms. F. can be reached at 555-555-5555. We are reaching out by phone to every second-grade family so that you can share with us whatever information you think we should know to help us be the best teacher of your child this year. Please expect to hear from us regularly and feel free to contact us with your questions, concerns, and any "good news" you want to share. We ask that you not call us between the hours of 8:30 a.m. and 4:30 p.m. on school days, except for an emergency. Those are the hours we are with the children and it is extremely hard for us to shift our focus.

Starting today, our children are reading, writing, engaging in math, and talking together about how to build a second-grade community where each child learns a lot and enjoys his or her school experience. The "specials" we have in second grade are Science, Art, Physical Education, and "Playmakers," an activity-based period focused on joyful community-building. We will send out a schedule soon.

Please make sure to return your emergency card form right away so we have complete contact information for your child.

Thank you for your support!

WELCOME BACK!

I am delighted to be your child's U.S. History 2 teacher during this important academic year. I will work hard to provide students with opportunities to improve their reading, writing, and critical thinking skills.

We will be starting off the year by exploring the Industrial Revolution in America—an important part of which took place right here in Lowell! Then we will move on to learn about Labor Movements and Unions, the expansion West, the progressive era, and finally in November, tackling World War I!

I hope that I can get to know you and your family throughout the year. I have gone over the course information and expectations with our class, but I have asked students to go through our class information with you this evening.

Please let me know if you have questions.

I hope we can be in touch throughout the year. Attached is an invitation to sign up for the phone app "Remind." I hope you can sign up tonight. Remind will allow you to text me at any time if you have questions. I will also text updates, homework reminders, and pictures from our class.

I look forward to working with your child this year. I also look forward to meeting you and learning from you how best to support the growth of your child. Hopefully we can meet at the upcoming Parent's Night at the high school; I am also happy to meet you in your neighborhood.

If you have any questions or concerns, please contact me at any time. My email is: jlander@xxxxx.k12.xx.us. Please feel free to reach out at any time.

All the best,
Ms. Jessica Lander

Tool #4: Home Visit Log

The Parent Teacher Home Visiting Project has a wonderful collection of tools to support your work in reaching out to families. We urge you to check out their website to find a variety of helpful tools (www.pthvp.org/toolbox/toolbox-of-best-practices). One we wanted to highlight is a Home Visit Log that can support your reflective work after a home visit, and can help you organize the important things you learn about your families when you meet with them.

Home Visit Log			
Student's name	Family members	Address	Telephone/email
The call	Scheduled visit?	Date & time	Translator or colleague included?
First visit	Topics discussed	New knowledge	Follow-up needed?
Second visit	Topics discussed	New knowledge	Follow-up needed?
End-of-year evaluation	Improvements in behavior, attendance, or academics?	Parent support with homework or more visible at school?	Suggestions for next year?

Tool #5: Ten Steps to Success for Developing School-Family Compacts

The School-Parent Compact Project (http://ctschoolparentcompact.org) strives to foster partnerships between families and schools with a focus on setting shared academic goals. The initiative and corresponding website is sponsored by the Connecticut Department of Education, and the site provides a wealth of resources, including a 10-step process (that you can download at http://ctschoolparentcompact.org/wp-content/uploads/2011/06/Tool_1A.pdf) that describes how to go about setting up these compacts and goals with families, and how you can help your whole school get on board.

More Tools to Build Partnerships With Families

We also suggest that you check out Chapter 11, "Tools That Support Your Work," from *Beyond the Bake Sale: The Essential Guide to Family-School Partnerships* **(2007). The chapter includes 12 sample tools such as a homework and school climate survey.**

Additional Organizations and Resources

Strong family engagement requires the support and work of the whole community. There are a wide array of organizations and resources doing this essential work that can support the work you do in your individual classrooms. Whether your school is just starting out on this journey or already a full-blown partnership school, having the help and ideas of great organizations well versed in strategies and approaches will make your work more successful. We urge you to explore the following organizations and resources.

ABCD Toolkit, Northwest Regional Development Lab, authored by Diane Dorfman

http://www.abcdinstitute.org/docs/Diane%20Dorfman-Mapping-Community-Assets-WorkBook(1)-1.pdf

The ABCD Toolkit walks you through an intensive and thought-provoking exercise that helps you identify and chart the skills, talents, and knowledge of your community. Doing this gives you a visual image of the diversity in your school and family community.

Boston Basics

http://bostonbasics.org/about

The Boston Basics are five evidence-based parenting and caregiving principles that encompass much of what experts find is important for children from birth to age three. Every child from every background can benefit from routinely experiencing Boston Basics learning experiences. Therefore, the Boston Basics Initiative is working through a broad range of institutions to ensure that every parent and caregiver is fully supported by family and friends to use the Boston Basics practices in everyday life.

Families In Schools

https://www.familiesinschools.org

http://staging.familiesinschools.org/what-we-do/trainings/staff-professional-development

Families In Schools provides sustainable capacity-building professional development trainings and tools for teachers, offering modules on topics such as how to create welcoming and family-friendly environments and how to encourage and increase family participation. As they describe on their website: "For 16 years, Families In Schools has provided capacity building to schools and organizations to effectively empower and engage parents in supporting their child's education. Currently, FIS partners with over 400 schools and organizations state and nationwide to help families fulfill their role as their child's first teacher."

Flamboyan Foundation

http://flamboyanfoundation.org

The Flamboyan Foundation helps school leaders, teachers, and other school staff reach out in targeted, helpful ways to families. It also helps families better understand and respond to the behavioral and learning challenges their child experiences in the classroom. Working in collaboration with the District of Columbia School District, Flamboyan has engaged in a family engagement initiative in DCPS (D.C. Public Schools) that features home visits and Academic Parent Teacher Teams. National research combined with unique observations from educators and families has helped Flamboyan determine the five most significant aspects to helping any student overcome obstacles to success: setting high expectations, monitoring performance and holding children accountable, supporting learning at home, guiding children's education through college, and advocating for them. Their website offers Parent Teacher Conferences Resource Tools, a School-Wide Family Engagement Rubric, a Teacher Family Engagement Resource that includes tools for communicating with families about academic progress, and video testimonials from teachers, who share how this research-based mode of family engagement has markedly improved students' academic, social, and emotional well-being in the classroom.

Friday CAFE

http://fridaycafe.org

Judy Carson, director for school-family-community partnerships at the Connecticut State Department of Education, has found that often teachers and other educators working in family engagement struggle to make connections and create robust learning communities to share best practices. In response, she created the Friday CAFE (Community and Family Engagement)—a monthly Friday morning gathering for practitioners involved in family engagement work to network, engage, and share ideas and practices, including everyone from teachers, principals, school staff, and community organizations to social service leaders. Carson has structured the events to include a brief-centered conversation on a topic (e.g., Trust, Open-Door School, or Student Voice in Partnership), but allowing substantial time for discussion. The model is currently being replicated in districts across the country, with teachers finding times to create similar meet-ups after classroom hours.

Harvard Family Research Project

http://www.hfrp.org

The Harvard Family Research Project (HFRP) evaluates and shares strategies that support children at home, at school, and in the larger community. HFRP has a number of resources and tools for families to depend on, including making the latest research accessible and available for families. Their research is created primarily with the goal of providing practical ideas that can be implemented swiftly. Focal areas of research include Family Involvement, Out-of-School Time, Learning with Data, Early Care and Education, and Evaluation. You can sign up for their FINE newsletters, which regularly deliver research-based information about family engagement as well as offer teaching tools, training materials, and research reports. Other resources available at the HFRP site include writings on Parent-Teacher Communication, Teacher Preparation and Professional Development, Cultural Diversity, Evaluating Family Involvement, and Research on Why Family Involvement Matters.

Institute for Educational Leadership

http://iel.org/fce

The Institute for Educational Leadership seeks to provide equal opportunity for all children and youth to learn, develop, and become contributing citizens. IEL helps influence policy makers, administrators, and practitioners through their leadership development and professional development programs. Their programs include leadership, policy, and networking experiences for a variety of professionals, such as educators in early childhood development, K–12 and higher education, and children- and youth-related policy. Though this site is geared more toward community schools and older students, resources for teachers include an individualized Learning Plan Guide to assist with college and career readiness; the Community Schools Scaling Up Guide, which provides practice and research for the benefits and practical ways of expanding community schools to be system-wide; and resources documenting the importance of early childhood education, among many other resources.

National Association for Family, School, and Community Engagement

http://nafsce.org

The National Association for Family, School, and Community Engagement (NAFSCE), founded in September 2014, is the first membership association focused solely on advancing family, school, and community engagement (FSCE). NAFSCE was established to provide the long-needed platform for advancing high-impact practices, promoting evidence-based policies, building capacity and leadership in the field, and upholding FSCE as a core strategy for improving child development and student achievement. NAFSCE provides networking opportunities to share ideas for effective practices. Resources include webinars, convenings, summary explanations of federal, state, and district policies about creating family-school partnerships, and a publications archive for research and reports.

Parents as Teachers

http://www.parentsasteachers.org

Parents as Teachers is both a resource and a network of organizations and professionals. At Parents as Teachers, training is available to educators, child-care providers, and healthcare providers to assist parents with preparing their children for the future. The pillars of what PAT does include develop curricula, train professionals to address a child's developmental needs and help to provide parents with real solutions for real-world situations, advocate for children and families, and set high standards through evidence-based research. Parents as Teachers offers a home visiting model that can be implemented through a choice of in-person seminars, a customized on-site session for staff, or distance learning. There are resources on the website, such as a page of fact sheets offering information on various topics such as diversity in families, health care, and affordable housing.

Parent Teacher Association (PTA) Family Engagement Tools

http://www.pta.org

This website offers a number of ways parents can be involved in their children's education. Families are the intended audience, but there are plenty of ideas and tools on this website that teachers can benefit from. The "Family Engagement Tools" section provides a link to the Diversity & Inclusion Toolkit, a downloadable PDF showing how to strengthen communities through representing all different types of people in terms of age, ethnicity, gender, language and culture, and socioeconomic status; the Smart Talk Toolkit—with accompanying videos—which helps to facilitate clear conversations about all the devices used today and how to be responsible using them; the Every Child in Focus tools, which include access to live webinars featuring a leadership series; and the Family Reading Experience tool, with resources to inspire both parents and educators to explore different ways to inspire children to read.

Parent Teacher Home Visit Project

http://www.pthvp.org

The Parent Teacher Home Visit Project advocates for relational family home visits, like the kind we describe in Chapter 3. The PTHV model is created on relationship building between teachers and families so that everyone can do his or her part to meet the needs of the child. Teachers are trained and compensated for their time, meetings are planned in advance, and after the first meeting, visits are consistently made by pairs of teachers. PTHV offers a variety of research, case studies, and testimonials about how their model has helped to achieve the hopes and dreams families have for their children. They've received accolades for their work, which includes training, cultural connections, and a toolbox for best practices, among other offerings.

Right Question Institute

http://rightquestion.org

The Right Question Institute (RQI) is a nonprofit educational organization that provides a strategy for supporting those in low- and moderate-income communities. RQI has two objectives: to help people advocate for themselves no matter their level of education, and to promote "micro-democracy"— where ordinary encounters with public agencies are opportunities for individual citizens to "act democratically" and participate effectively in decisions that affect them. They work with families and communities to think about the types of information they want and how to get that information through formulating powerful questions. On their website you can find their Question Formulation Technique (QFT). Through membership in their Educator's Network, you can gain access to teaching strategies and a wealth of other resources. They offer teacher training as well as professional development through seminars and on-site visits. Resources include publications on education, health care, school-family partnership, and democracy, in the form of books, articles, blog posts, and research.

School-Parent Compact Project

http://ctschoolparentcompact.org

The School-Parent Compact Project was created with the goal of engaging families in their children's lives as students. Teachers and students design a School-Parent blueprint for action that links to their school's School Improvement Plan. SPCP provides a 10-step process that includes planning forms, templates, and sample documents to help create a School-Parent Contract. Training for this method of family engagement involves a series of workshops. Tools for this 10-step process are available for download on the site, as are some supplemental articles about educational leadership, the formation of family-school-community partnerships to advance student learning, and the School Parent Compact Program in a presentation for the U.S. Department of Education.

Teaching for Change

http://www.teachingforchange.org

Teaching for Change is an organization that provides teachers and parents with tools to create schools where students learn not just how to read and write, but also to question and rethink the world inside and outside their classrooms. The work at this organization is social- and history-based, and the site is largely focused on helping teachers teach children about the multicultural stories in history that are often glazed over and not explored in depth. They offer a variety of curricula for learning about and respecting differences in culture and race. Curricula include Anti-Bias Education, Zinn Education Project, Civil Rights Teaching, Teaching Central America, Teach the Beat: Go-Go Goes to School, and Teaching about Haiti. There are additional resources, including published articles, book lists, and video testimonials.

Professional Development Opportunities

Family Engagement in Education: Creating Effective Home and School Partnerships for Student Success

https://www.gse.harvard.edu/ppe

This three-and-a-half-day summer institute at the Harvard Graduate School of Education is designed to prepare participants to establish a culture and practices that genuinely honor and respect the knowledge that families bring to school improvement. Participants learn what it takes to design family engagement strategies that are directly connected to student learning. The institute faculty director is Karen Mapp, and sessions are taught and led by Harvard faculty as well as district and community leaders.

HarvardX MOOC: Introduction to Family Engagement in Education

http://online-learning.harvard.edu/course/introduction-family-engagement-education

Working with HarvardX—Harvard University's online Course/MOOC platform—Karen has created a six-week free course on the essentials of family engagement. Spending an average two to four hours a week, you will learn about the research linking family engagement to better educational outcomes, and hear directly from educators, students, and families about promising practices in the field.

National Network of Partnership Schools (NNPS)

http://nnps.jhucsos.com

Established at Johns Hopkins University in 1996, NNPS invites schools, districts, states, and organizations to join together and use research-based approaches to organize and sustain excellent programs of family and community involvement that will increase student success in school. Researchers and facilitators at the Center on School, Family, and Community Partnerships at Johns Hopkins University work with the members of NNPS to study the nature and results of involvement. NNPS aims to increase knowledge of new concepts and strategies; use research results to develop tools and materials that will improve policy and practice; provide professional development conferences and workshops; share best practices of parental involvement and community connections; and recognize excellent partnership programs at the school, district, organization, and state levels.

Dr. Karen Mapp's Family Engagement Workshop Series

http://teacher.scholastic.com/products/face/face-workshop.html

Scholastic FACE has created three different full-day interactive workshops based around Karen's work in Family Engagement. The workshops focus on exploring the link between family and community engagement and student achievement, with the goal of raising the power of family engagement and building a yearlong action plan to ensure continued success. The workshops are centered around the following three themes: "Redesigning Family Engagement: The Essential Ingredients," "Designing Family Engagement Events," and "Engaging Families Through Learning Throughout the Year." Each workshop includes access to a range of online videos and resources as well as access to consultative support.

Additional Books and Articles

Between Families and Schools: Teaching for Change
www.teachingforchange.org/parent-organizing/between-families

Beyond Bedtime Stories: A Parent's Guide to Promoting Reading, Writing, and Other Literacy Skills From Birth to 5 by V. Susan Bennett-Armistead, Nell Duke, and Annie Moses (Scholastic)

Con Respeto: An Ethnography About the Relationship Between Mexican Families and the Local Schools www.amazon.com/Respeto-Bridging-Distances-Culturally-Ethnographic/dp/0807735264

Engage Every Family: Five Simple Principles by Steve Constantino (Corwin Press)

Innovation Brief: Reaching & Supporting Families Where They Are
Campaign for Grade Level Reading. http://api.ning.com/files/pezQEPsid2 gG3eq1geqZqvadWBRNUuw2vLFiibgXpjDvhJr Ulwm65KEpzpIgqvkGGyZ9P8c EvNUQs6ACLzlDQEln993Au LQC/4InnovationBriefReachingSupporting Parents.pdf

"Making the Most of School-Family Compacts" Schools, Families, Communities, pages 48–53. *Education Leadership*. May 2011 | Volume 68 | Number 8. By Anne T. Henderson, Judy Carson, Patti Avallone, and Melissa Whipple. www.ascd.org/publications/educational_leadership/may11/vol68/ num08/Making_the_Most_of_School-Family_Compacts.aspx

Ordinary Magic This book discusses the literature of resilience in children and adolescents and reinforces the importance of the "one caring other" in changing the trajectory of children who are at risk. www.amazon.com/ Ordinary-Magic-Development-Ann-Masten-ebook/dp/B00LLMLXNY/ref=sr_1_1 ?s=books&ie=UTF8&qid=1477880974&sr=8-1&keywords=ordinary+magic

Partnering with Parents to Ask the Right Questions: A Powerful Strategy for Strengthening School-Family Partnerships by Luz Santana, Dan Rothstein, and Agnes Bain (ASCD)

School, Family, and Community Partnerships: Your Handbook for Action, 3rd Edition, by Joyce L. Epstein and Associates (Corwin)

Tapping the Potential of Parents: A Strategic Guide to Boosting Student Achievement Through Family Involvement by Patricia Edwards (Scholastic)

Unequal Childhoods by Annette Lareau. www.ucpress.edu/book.php?isbn= 9780520271425

Classroom Tools

Guide to the Boston Public School for Families and Students

http://www.bostonpublicschools.org/cms/lib07/MA01906464/Centricity/Domain/187/BPS%20Guide%20SY16%20English.pdf

This guide, published in 10 languages, provides information to families on school policies, education resources, advocating for your child, and opportunities for family involvement. There is a section that is focused on how schools engage families with student learning, and tips for parents on how they can support their children's learning at home. Teachers in Boston are encouraged not simply to pass this out to families, but to use the guides as a conversation starter about grade level goals and ways that teachers and the students' families can work together to achieve those goals.

Scholastic Literacy Events

http://teacher.scholastic.com/products/face/literacy-events.html

Literacy Events kits for Pre-K to Grade 5 are Scholastic's innovative approach to promoting family engagement—an important component in a child's education—that builds capacity, creates a shared responsibility for educational success, provides tools and the confidence to use them, and lets educational leaders develop strong home, school, and community partnerships.

Teaching for Tolerance

http://www.tolerance.org

The Teaching for Tolerance program has many great resources for teachers, such as a "Let's Talk" booklet to help educators enter conversations about race. www.tolerance.org/lets-talk

The National Education Association

http://www.nea.org

The NEA, the nation's largest professional employee organization, has some good resources for teachers and parents, including their Diversity Toolkit. www.nea.org/tools/diversity-toolkit.html

Evaluation Tools

Family-School Relationships Survey

https://www.panoramaed.com/family-school-relationships-survey

Schools can use the Family-School Relationships Survey to gather feedback while effectively engaging parents and guardians. Developing parents' capacity to contribute to their children's learning is an important factor in promoting positive student outcomes.

Designed as a series of scales—groups of questions that capture different aspects of the same underlying theme—the Family-School Relationships Survey provides educators flexibility in measuring an array of aspects of parent attitudes. The survey is designed to be used by principals, district staff, school boards, state departments of education, or parent-teacher organizations. The survey can be administered to any K–12 school community (public, private, independent, charter, urban, or rural) and has already been used by thousands of schools nationwide. The survey is available in 10 additional languages, including Spanish, Portuguese, and Mandarin.

Massachusetts Educator Evaluator Standards

http://www.doe.mass.edu/edeval/model/PartIII_AppxC.pdf

These standards offer an example of a state rubric that incorporates family engagement as a core proficiency standard for teachers, school leaders, and superintendents. (See pages C10 and C11.)

PTA: National Standards for Family and School Partnerships

http://www.pta.org/nationalstandards

The National Parent Teacher Association (PTA) has created a series of six standards and measures to help define what powerful family engagement looks like. In addition to this set of national standards, they include a series of resources and tools to help build schools' and teachers' capacities.

REFERENCES

Alexander, K. (2016). *Kwame Alexander's page-to-stage writing workshop: Awakening the writer, publisher, and presenter in every student.* New York: Scholastic.

Allensworth, E., Ponisciak, S., & Mazzeo, C. (2009). *The schools teachers leave: Teacher mobility in Chicago public schools.* Retrieved from ERIC database (505882).

Boser, U. (2011). *Teacher diversity matters: A state-by-state analysis of teachers of color.* Retrieved from the Center for American Progress website: www.americanprogress.org/issues/education/reports/2011/11/09/10657/teacher-diversity-matters.

Bryk, A. S. (2010). *Organizing schools for improvement: Lessons from Chicago.* Chicago: University of Chicago Press.

Dabkowski, D. W. (2004). Encouraging active parent participation in IEP team meetings. *Teaching Exceptional Children, 36*(3), 34–39.

Gill Kressley, K. (August, 2008). *Breaking new ground: Seeding proven practices into proven programs.* National PIRC Conference, Baltimore, MD.

González, N., Moll, L. C., & Amanti, C. (2005). *Funds of knowledge: Theorizing practice in households, communities, and classrooms.* Mahwah, NJ: L. Erlbaum Associates.

Henderson, A. T. and Mapp, K. L. (2002). *A new wave of evidence: The impact of school, family, and community connections on student achievement.* National Center for Family and Community Connections with Schools, Southwest Educational Development Laboratory.

Henderson, A. T., Mapp, K. L., Johnson, V. R., & Davies, D. (2007). *Beyond the bake sale: The essential guide to family-school partnerships.* New York: The New Press.

Higgins, M. C. (2005). *Career imprints: Creating leaders across an industry.* San Francisco: Jossey-Bass.

Hong, S. (manuscript in preparation, 2016). *Natural Allies: Voices of Teachers Committed to Families.* Harvard Education Press, Cambridge, MA.

Hong, S. (manuscript in preparation, 2016). *Relearning Families: Teachers Challenge Myths about Parent–Teacher Relationships.*

Hoover-Dempsey, K., Walker, J.M.T., & Sandler, H. M. (2005). Why do parents become involved? Research findings and implications. *Elementary School Journal, 106*(2), 105–130. doi:10.1086/499194.

Lawrence-Lightfoot, S. (2003). *The essential conversation: What parents and teachers can learn from each other.* New York: Random House.

Lopez, G. R. (2001). The value of hard work: Lessons on parent involvement from an (im)migrant household. *Harvard Educational Review, 71*(3), 416–437.

Mapp, K. L. (2003). Having their say: Parents describe why and how they are engaged in their children's learning. *School Community Journal, 13*(1), 35–64.

Mapp, K. & Kuttner, P. (2014). *Partners in education: A dual capacity-building framework for family-school partnerships.* Austin, TX: Southwest Educational Development Laboratory.

Markow, D., & Pieters, A. (2009). *The MetLife survey of the American teacher: Collaborating for student success.* New York: MetLife.

Moll, L., Amanti, C., Neff, D., & González, N. (2005). Funds of knowledge for teaching: Using a qualitative approach to connect homes and classrooms. In *Funds of Knowledge: Theorizing Practices in Households, Communities, and Classrooms.* (pp. 71–88). Lawrence Erlbaum Associates.

Principles of Adult Learning. (n.d.). Retrieved November 27, 2016, from www.literacy.ca/professionals/professional-development-2/principles-of-adult-learning.

Tatum, B. D. (2003). *"Why are all the black kids sitting together in the cafeteria?": And other conversations about race.* New York: Basic Books.

Warren, M. R., Mapp, K. L., & Kuttner, P. (2015). From private citizens to public actors: The development of parent leaders through community organizing. In M. P. Evans & D. B. Hiatt Michael (Eds.), *The power of community engagement for educational change.* (pp. 21–39). Charlotte, NC: Information Age Publishing, Inc.

Valencia, R. R. (Ed.) (1997). *The evolution of deficit thinking: Educational thought and practice.* London: Falmer Press.

Zacarian, D. (2011). *Transforming schools for English learners: A comprehensive framework for school leaders.* Thousand Oaks, CA: Corwin Press.

VIDEO PARTNERSHIP CLIPS

The following videos can be accessed at **scholastic.com/PartnerResources**. You may want to watch them on your own as you explore each chapter and also review them in staff meetings when you are discussing policies for interacting with students' families.

Your Colleagues Reflect (Interviews With Educators)

Dr. Mapp's Harvard Online Course and Presentations

INDEX